Wandering in Norfolk

Wandering in Norfolk

Time Lines and Crossing Places

David Howe

Wandering in Norfolk

Time Lines and Crossing Places

First published in 2016

by:

Mousehold Press
6, Constitution Opening
Norwich, NR3 4BD
www.mousehold-press.co.uk

Maps by Terry Loan

ISBN 978-1-874739-80-7

Printed by Page Bros (Norwich)

Contents

List of Illustrations   vii

Maps   viii

Chapter 1   Ice and Rock   11

Chapter 2   Pebbles and Posts   21

Chapter 3   Mass and Energy   32

Chapter 4   Chalk and Flint   41

Chapter 5   Rights and Wrongs   57

Chapter 6   Walkers and Wonderers   67

Chapter 7   Sand and Sea   79

                   Picture Section

Chapter 8   Sailors and Sinners   89

Chapter 9   Invaders and Insurgents   106

Chapter 10   Wool and Wealth   120

Chapter 11   Rascals and Radicals   139

Chapter 12   Tracks and Trails   162

Chapter 13   Love and Life   182

Chapter 14   The Brief and The Beautiful   196

Acknowledgements   211

Bibliography   213

For Jacob and Rebecca, Norfolk bred,
Matt, Norfolk born,
and Angela

Illustrations

Plate 1   Albert Einstein: painting on promenade café wall, Sheringham

Plate 2   Albert Einstein by his hut on Roughton Heath

Plate 3   Hunstanton: Chalk and Carstone cliffs

Plate 4   Hunstanton cliffs: close up

Plate 5   Sir Thomas Browne: statue, Hay Hill, Norwich

Plate 6   Blakeney Point

Plate 7   Holkham Beach

Plate 8   ALBATROS: sailing clipper, Wells-next-the Sea

Plate 9   Nelson: statue, precincts of Norwich Cathedral

Plate 10   North Elmham, remains of Norman Chapel

Plate 11   Remains of Roman market town, Caistor St Edmund

Plate 12   Round towered church, St Andrew, Colney

Plate 13   Amelia Opie, figurine statue, Opie Street, Norwich

Plate 14   Robert Kett, bronze roundel, Norwich City Hall

Plate 15   Kett's Oak, B1172, near Wymondham, Norfolk

Plate 16   Thomas Paine, statue, King Street, Thetford

Plate 17   Hickling Broad and Heigham Sound

Plate 18   B1113 road between Redgrave and South Lopham, the watershed between the source of the River Waveney and the Little Ouse River

Plate 19   Margaret Fountaine

Plate 20   Julian of Norwich, statue, West Door, Norwich Cathedral

Plate 21   Igneous erratics on Cromer beach

Plate 22   'Flint squared' and 'flint knapped random' walls

Plate 23   Norfolk sky

Norfolk – towns and rivers

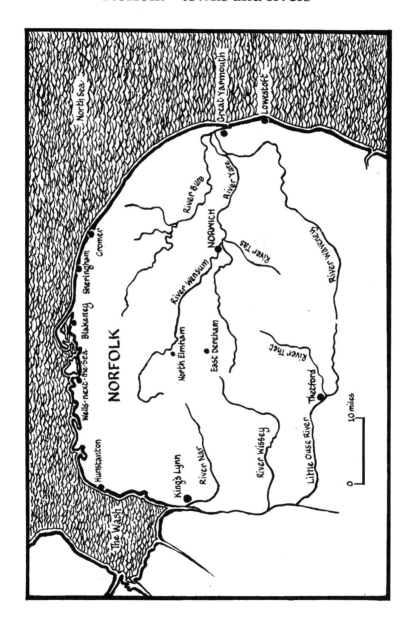

Norfolk – geology

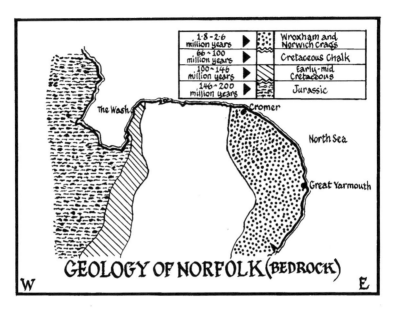

1.8 - 2.6 million years	▶		Wroxham and Norwich Crags
66 - 100 million years	▶		Cretaceous Chalk
100 - 146 million years	▶		Early - mid Cretaceous
146 - 200 million years	▶		Jurassic

GEOLOGY OF NORFOLK (BEDROCK)

W   E

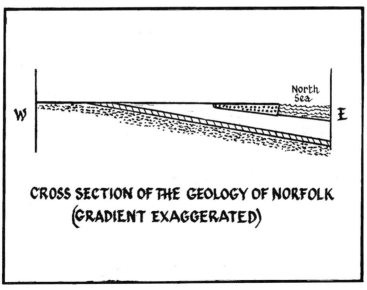

CROSS SECTION OF THE GEOLOGY OF NORFOLK
(GRADIENT EXAGGERATED)

Chapter 1
Ice and Rocks

I'm standing on a hill. Beacon Hill. At a height of 338 feet it is the highest point in Norfolk. Not very high, admittedly, but it gives the lie to Noel Coward's claim, made in his play *Private Lives* and often quoted, 'Very flat, Norfolk.' No it's not, Noel. Well not *very*.

Of course, it is true that Norfolk doesn't have too many ups and downs. On a hot summer's day in 1976, not long after I had moved to Norfolk, I was at Norwich station and saw a young man, maybe a relation of Mr Coward, wearing a tee-shirt announcing that he was a member of the 'Norfolk Mountain Rescue Club'. I was about to catch the train for Great Yarmouth. The plan was to walk along the coast to Winterton.

This marked the beginning of my Norfolk wanderings, wanderings that turned out to be geographical and historical, scientific and philosophical. I wandered in thought as well as on foot. I followed the invisible threads that run between people and the places where they live, the past and present. And of course I roamed the county's ups and downs.

I first came across the word geomorphology as a teenager. I loved the sound of it and what it defined – *geomorphology*. Geo – morph – ology, the study of land forms. As an even younger boy I would draw maps of imaginary countries, usually islands, with contours and streams, roads and railways, towns and cities. I pored over atlases, looking up longest rivers, highest mountains, countries, capital cities, that sort of thing. I was that kind of kid.

Anyway, here are a few geomorphological, or more specifically topographical facts about Norfolk and its East Anglian neighbours that I thought you'd like to know; ought to know. The highest point in Suffolk, the county immediately to the south of Norfolk is Great Wood Hill which beats Beacon Hill by a few feet, topping out at 420 feet. Great Chishill in Cambridgeshire to the east is 479 feet high, while only a mile away across the county border is Chrishall Common in Essex which reaches the dizzy, albeit flattish height of 482 feet. Honesty requires me to tell you that these four counties possess the four lowest highest points (concentrate) of any of the counties in the British Isles. This means that the whole of East Anglia, if not flat, is, at best, described as undulating.

Beacon Hill lies just south of the village of West Runton, roughly half way between Cromer and Sheringham. I'm on the North Norfolk coast looking out to sea. This raised area is part of the Cromer Ridge that runs for nearly 20 miles from Mundesley in the east to Langham in the west. Its sands, gravels and clays were left behind by the melting, retreating, thousands of feet thick, Anglian ice sheet over 400,000 years ago. The Ridge is a terminal moraine, a hilly reminder of chilly times long ago, softened by time. Although much of the hill is covered in woodland and scrub, there is a view down to the coast, a mile away.

Part of this hilly area is also known as Roman Camp. This is rather fanciful, although there are some small circular earth works on the summit. The story goes that in the early 19th century, local horse-drawn cab drivers, keen to boost the beginnings of the Georgian tourist trade, decided to add a bit of romance to the area. The rough, not terribly convincing diggings, they said, were the remains of a camp and look-out site built by the Romans. So ran their patter. 'Rather than take the direct road from Cromer to Sheringham', they said, 'Why not take the scenic route? Why not visit the Roman ruins? Only a short detour. Hardly cost you.'

What is less in dispute is that Beacon Hill was the location of an old coastal signalling station. It was certainly there in the early 19th century at the time of the Napoleonic Wars. Earlier still, the spot was an obvious place to keep an eye on what was happening along the coast and out at sea. Old 18th century maps make mention of *The Old Beacon*, or sometimes the *Watch Tower*. Worries about invasions from the Dutch in the 1650s led to monies being raised to keep these coastal look-out towers in good repair.

Beacon Hill might not have been a place where Roman soldiers were stationed but the gentle rise does attract 21st century Roman campers. A few feet below the hill on the south side is the Roman Camp Caravan Park featuring chalets and static caravans. I'm not sure if you can actually see the sea from this park but you are surrounded by National Trust woodland and a sense of history, albeit some of a spurious nature.

Many paths and tracks wander the area. Today I'm taking one that winds down through woods and fields to the small coastal town of West Runton. As I walk the slipway on to the sand and pebbles I notice a large crowd and a TV camera crew. In the middle of the melée is the outline of a very large, thirteen foot tall bamboo and pine framed elephant. Strapped to each leg is a person. And when each person begins to walk in some clever choreographed sequence, the jointed, articulated elephant comes to life as it trundles slowly along the beach, cheered on by the crowd.

The elephant was built by the aircraft engineer, Jeremy Moore with help from Ali MacKenzie of Tin House Arts. It is their tribute to the great West Runton Elephant.

Winter 1990. After a spell of stormy weather, local residents Harold and Margaret Hems took a walk along the beach looking for fossils. Heavy rain and big waves regularly wash away the soft base of the West Runton cliffs. Every now and again, the ancient sediments release a long held prisoner of time. And so it was that on 13 December, Harold and Margaret were excited to find a large bone sticking out of the silts and sands.

Being a responsible pair, they alerted Norfolk Museum Services who decided to take a look. The experts quickly realised that the fossil was the pelvic bone of a large male elephant-like creature. A year later and another December storm and yet more elephant bones were washed to the surface.

North Norfolk appears to be blessed with keen-eyed, knowledgeable, beach combing citizens. The new bones were spotted by Rob Sinclair and again Norfolk Museum Services were contacted. It was by now apparent that these new bones were part of the same elephant-like skeleton that Harold and Margaret had found, the bulk of which presumably still lay buried under the cliffs. With the help of Cromer Museum and a number of volunteers, roughly a quarter of the bones of this large beast were recovered. But tantalisingly, it was obvious that there was much more of the animal still entombed deep within the cliffs.

Funded by grants from the Heritage Lottery and Anglian Water, in 1995 it was decided to mount a project to excavate the whole of the elephant. This involved removing thousands of tons of sand, silt and gravel. Two weeks after the digging had begun, first one bone appeared, then another, until eventually by November of that year, an almost complete skeleton had been unearthed, including a massive skull and a pair of huge curly tusks. One of the leg bones alone was almost the length of a man.

There he had lain for almost 700,000 years, *Mammuthus trogontherii*, the largest mammal ever to have walked on land. He was 41 years old when he died. Standing 4 metres tall and weighing 10 tons, this steppe mammoth was twice the size of the modern African elephant and larger than the mammoths of Wrangel Island which lies off the coast of north east Siberia. These Siberian mammoths were some of the last ever survivors of their species, dying out a mere 4,000 years ago. But here, on a light breezy summer's day, *Mammuthus trogontherii*, could be seen once again, swaying gently along Weston Runton beach, guided with loving care by Jeremy and his friends.

The mammoth was not alone in his muddy grave. His bones were found in the West Runton Freshwater Beds, which in turn are a member of the Cromer Forest Bed Formation. Around 700,000 years ago the so called 'Ancaster River' was postulated to flow down from the Pennines out along what is the current North Norfolk Coast out into the sea. As it did so, fresh and brackish organic sands, silts and muds were deposited. The sediments were laid down when this part of the world was a constantly changing landscape of plains, rivers, lakes, brackish waters, shallow seas, and, as the name suggests, trees and forests. The range of bones and other fossil remains that have been found in these soft rocks is quite remarkable.

OK, most are just tiny fragments and very small, but dozens and dozens of species have been identified. Here are just a few. As well as plant and pollen remains, shells of many varieties wash out of the muds. There are freshwater fish of many kinds. Newts and frogs. Snakes. Ducks, thrushes, moorhens, crows and many other birds. Shrews, moles, and hedgehogs. Hares and squirrels, otters and beavers. A bear. A spotted hyaena. Deer and elks, little horses and big horses, boar and a bison. A sabre tooth tiger and a lion! A rhino for heavens sake. And of course a mammoth. Isn't that extraordinary? All swimming, scurrying, sniffing, stalking and stomping around this part of the world all that time ago.

Perhaps even more extraordinary, just along the coast going east, round the shoulder of Norfolk, humans were also wandering across the plains and along the river banks around roughly the same time. In May 2013, human footprints over 800,000 years old were discovered at Happisburgh. They are the oldest known human footprints to have been found outside Africa. The sea had washed away beach sands to expose about fifty impressions of feet both large and small. They revealed themselves in a layer of ancient muddy estuarine silts only visible at low tide. But the soft muddy silts, previously protected by sand and water, were now prey to the tides.

Two weeks later they had vanished, washed away by the sea, but not before a team of scientists from the British Museum had studied and photographed them in 3D.

Subsequent analysis revealed the footprints to be those of several adults and a number of children, walking south across the muddy flats of an ancient river estuary. A family perhaps? But the imprints were not made by our own species, *homo sapiens*, 'man who knows'. We didn't make our appearance on the Earth until around 200,000 years ago in what is now modern north east Africa. These much older Happisburgh footprints were possibly made by a now extinct species of human, *homo antecessor* or 'Pioneer Man', similar in height and physique to modern humans but with slightly smaller heads and a tinier brain size. And there the little family roamed, hunting and gathering over the wide open valleys and river estuaries of Norfolk a hundred thousand years before the West Runton mammoth met its fate.

Back on West Runton beach, the crowds, the cameras and the mammoth have now turned around. They are making their way back to the slipway. I carry on walking towards Cromer leaving the elephant behind. It is suddenly quiet. I stop for a moment between the flat, blue-grey sea and the soft, grey-brown cliffs. I'm on a beach, in Norfolk, on the eastern fringes of a relatively small island, anchored off the north western edge of Europe, 53° North, where, nearly a million years before, life teemed. The pebbles and sand stretch empty in the distance. The breeze has dropped and the line between sea and sky has all but disappeared in the late afternoon haze. There is something compelling about wide spaces and wild places. Untamed landscapes diminish and thrill us in equal measure.

At the base of the cliffs, beneath the glacial tills and the odd massive raft of chalk, lies a thin outcrop of black-brown, muddy-looking rock that disappears beneath the beach. These are the Cromer Forest Beds in a section of which the mammoth was found. These soft rocks were laid down over several hundred thousand years between, roughly, 850,000 and 450,000 years ago. Standing on the beach today by the crumbling cliffs, it is hard to imagine that when the mammoth and his friends were wandering the land, there were no cliffs, no waves washing the shore, no North Sea as we know it today. Norfolk and beyond was then an open, flat plain veined by rivers that meandered slowly east out into a distant shallow sea. There were estuaries fringed by grasses and trees. The climate was warm. But, every so often, these balmy times came to a shivering halt.

Every few hundred million years, planet Earth chills and suffers a major Ice Age. There have been at least five over the last two or three billion years. The biggest and baddest was the Cryogenean Ice Age also known, Hollywood style, as Snowball Earth. All this happened around 700 to 800 million years ago. So severe was the cooling that ice sheets spread further and further south in the north, and further and further north in the south, until they almost reached the equator. It's hard to imagine.

The most recent of the major Ice Ages, known as the Quaternary, was in fact, geologically speaking, very recent. Technically, this is the one in which we still find ourselves today. It's the one that has shaped the landscape of the British Isles as we currently know it, including that of Norfolk. This latest Ice Age began about two and a half million years ago and it defines the present major Geological Era.

What causes Ice Ages is still a matter of debate. Likely culprits include changes in the Earth's orbit and axis around the sun, the angle at which the sun's rays strike the surface at particular latitudes, the Earth's 22,000 year cyclical wobble, the movement and position of the continents caused by plate tectonics, how the ocean's currents switch and swirl between and around continents, how active the world's volcanoes happen to be at any one time, and how much or how little carbon dioxide and methane there is in the atmosphere. It's likely that there are complex interactions between all these elements and when two or more come together, temperatures drop, the snows fall, the summers get colder so less snow melts, glaciers grow and ice sheets spread. And just over two million years ago one of these chilling configurations began to take shape.

To complicate matters further, during any one major Ice Age, there can be a number of warm bursts. These interglacial warm phases can last tens of thousands of years, sandwiched between the long, very cold spells. Over the last two and a half million years, the Quaternary ice sheets have therefore waxed and waned many times.

Today, we are in one of the relatively warm interglacial periods, but with the distinct possibility that another cold glacial spell will sweep the planet in the next thirty odd thousand years, although of course man-made global warming is the new joker in the Earth-history pack and who knows quite what might happen next.

In Britain and Northern Europe, the biggest of these Quaternary ice advances happened around 450,000 years ago. It is known as The Anglian Ice Sheet. Its effects can be studied across much of Britain including East Anglia. The end of this ice mass reached as far south as the current Thames and Severn valleys in a line running roughly between London and Bristol.

I continue heading east towards Cromer. Again I stop and look up at the cliffs. They tumble untidily seaward occasionally revealing house-size blocks of white chalk buried in the glacial sands and silts. The massive ice sheets had the power to gouge and scoop huge chunks of chalk from the bedrock below and carry them east and south. When the ice melted and retreated, these massive 'ice rafts' of chalk were dumped along with all the other glacial debris. They were left high and dry buried in the silts, sands and clays until erosion by wind, rain and sea once again exposed them, stranded, walls of white trapped amongst the pale yellows and dirty greys of the surrounding glacial detritus.

During the Anglian ice advance, only the very south of the British Isles was ice free, but even here the land was cold and tundra-like. Standing where I am today on the northern flanks of Norfolk, several hundred metres of ice would have been piled above my head. But then slowly, once more, the planet began to warm, the ice melted, the snow sheets retreated, and the land re-appeared, having been scoured and scarred by the slow, relentless power of the moving ice.

If the Anglian glaciation was the biggest of the Quaternary ice advances, the most recent was the Devensian. The best evidence and rock debris associated with this ice sheet has been found on the banks of the River Dee along the Welsh Borders. The Romans called the Dee the *Deva* and the people who lived on its banks *Devenses*, hence Devensian.

This last Ice advance began, like all ice advances, when global temperatures once again began to plummet. In Northern Europe, the winter snows fell more heavily, especially over the mountains. The summers were no longer warm enough to melt the winter drifts. The snows compacted and slowly turned to ice and ice, like water, flows down hill but slowly, glacially slow.

Over the mountains of the Lake District, Wales, the Pennines, Scotland and Scandinavia the rivers of ice glided and ground their way down the valleys, out onto the plains, merging to form vast ice sheets. Under their own weight, the sheets spread out in all directions, covering much of the land and the North Sea Basin. At their most extensive, these Devensian ice sheets formed a wilderness of white from Ireland to Norway. More modest than some of its Quaternary predecessors, nevertheless it still covered the northern half of the British Isles, the North Sea and Scandinavia. It peaked around 18,000 years ago and its icy reach just about touched the northern fringes of Norfolk. Again, standing where I am today all those chilly years ago, I would be shivering on a cold perma-frosted plain. If I looked north, I would see cliffs of ice towering on the skyline just a few miles away, grinding ever closer.

Because the Devensian glaciation was the last to affect the British Isles, the evidence of its advance and retreat is the most complete of all the Quaternary ice advances. At its peak, there was so much water locked up in the huge ice cap that sea level was over 100 metres lower than it is today. There was no North Sea, only ice to the north and tundra to the south.

Then, about 18,000 years ago, the planet began to warm once again, slowly at first. The sub-arctic plains gradually turned from dry, cold tundra to thin, sparse grassland. This land, today drowned by the North Sea, has been named Doggerland. It formed a land bridge spanning west to east, joining the British Isles to mainland Europe. Plants and animals were free to spread unhindered over Germany, Denmark, the Netherlands, Belgium, France and across to England, Wales and Ireland. Then 12,000 years ago, the warming process received another boost. Doggerland turned lush and green.

Chapter 2
Pebbles and Posts

Initially, the retreating ice sheets continued to block the northerly flow of rivers and the summer melt waters. Ancient precursors of the Thames and other rivers were forced east to join the west running proto-Rhine, Meuse and Scheldt rivers as they flowed across the warming plains of what is now East Anglia and the southern North Sea. These powerful, swollen rivers merged and flooded south, eventually flowing along and scouring what is now the English Channel before heading out into the Atlantic Ocean.

More ice melted and the rivers continued to swell. The fertile flood plains warmed even more. Woodlands of oak and ash appeared. The land grew ever green as shrubs and grasses spread north chasing the retreating ice. Deer, boar and large oxen grazed, rooted and nibbled. Birds flew, swam and pecked. There were trout in the rivers. This was a rich, borderless country over which our Mesolithic ancestors hunted and gathered from Ireland to the plains of France and Germany, from Norfolk to the Netherlands.

In 1931, the Lowestoft trawler, the *Colinda*, was fishing 25 miles off the east Norfolk coast. As it hauled in its catch, the crew noticed a large clump of peat caught up in the nets. Set within the peat was a carved piece of deer antler, 21 centimetres long. The skipper of the boat, saltily named Pilgrim Lockwood, wasn't quite sure what they had found. On landing, he handed the carving to the ship's owner who in turn presented it to a friend, who consulted a colleague until eventually it found its way to the Norwich Museum.

The archaeologists identified the antler, with its sharp barbs, as a prehistoric spear or harpoon point. In honour of the trawler, the spear was named the Colinda Point. The Museum dated the carved antler, suggesting it had been fashioned some 6 to 10,000 years ago.

It confirmed the idea that when the ice sheets first retreated, the whole of the southern North Sea Basin was a land rich in grasses and game, lakes and fish, rivers and wildlife. For Mesolithic men and women, Doggerland was a land of plenty.

Marine archaeologists and trawlermen continue to find the remains of animals and artefacts, axes and adzes scattered across a land that once connected Britain and Mainland Europe and which was once a busy and happy hunting ground for our Stone Age ancestors. In fact the evidence suggests that these Mesolithic tribes were developing a range of sophisticated skills and practices. They made jewellery. They traded food and goods. They were learning to actively manage their environment rather than simply respond passively to what nature sent their way. Their culture was complex and their social life grew increasingly elaborate.

And still the temperatures kept on rising. More ice melted. The seas steadily rose working their way around the British Isles. The river plains of Doggerland slowly succumbed to the rising waters and the southern basin of the North Sea began to take on its modern shape. Britain once more was becoming an island, and the men and women, isolated from their mainland cousins, became the first true Britons.

For a short while the highest ground of Doggerland kept its head above water. This was Dogger Island. It was the last of the old Doggerland to disappear beneath the waves, 5,000 years ago. Dogger Bank, that sandy rise beneath the fish-rich, shallow North Sea, a hundred miles north of Cromer, is the island's watery grave. And just in case you were wondering, *Dogger* is an old Dutch word for fishing boat.

Rising seas drown and bury but they can also scour and exhume. John Lorimer was a beach comber. One of his combing haunts was the coastal sands at Holme next the Sea, north-east of Hunstanton, thirty odd miles west of Cromer. In spring 1998 John found a Bronze Age axe head. Then, on a return search and to his surprise, he came across a large, apparently up-turned tree trunk sticking out of the low tidal waters. It looked very odd and out of place. Later visits revealed yet more buried post-shaped tree trunks. It gradually became apparent that the emerging posts formed a circle, nearly seven metres in diameter, around the large, central up-turned tree trunk. The ever-keen, ever-helpful Castle Museum in Norwich agreed to take a look at this curious beach find.

The Museum asked one of the county's archaeologists, Edwin Rose, to meet John and examine the strange circle of wooden posts. Edwin's initial thought was that the posts might be Anglo-Saxon fish traps, but he wasn't sure. So he contacted English Heritage who decided to carry out a full excavation beginning in 1999.

Samples of the wood sent to Sheffield University established that the structure was of Early Bronze Age, dating back about 4,000 years ago. The posts were dug into what originally would have been salt marshes surrounded by sand dunes and mudflats. Stone axes had been used to fell and shape the timber. In total, 55 oak posts, 3 metres long, were sunk a metre into what were then marsh silts forming a circle around the very large inverted base of the centrally placed tree trunk.

The people who built the circle were farmers. They grew wheat and barley, and grazed sheep and cattle. They lived in wooden round houses with walls made of wattle and daub, and roofs of timber thatched with reeds.

Over the centuries, the area where they had built the circle changed from salt marsh to waterlogged wetland. The Bronze Age farmers moved further inland. The 55 wooden posts and pivotal tree trunk became buried under layers of peat. Boggy peats are anaerobic. They lack oxygen and this helps preserve anything organic, including wooden posts, which finds itself buried beneath the decaying vegetation.

The sea though, was never very far away. Water levels, then as now, carried on rising. The sea encroached further inland, washing away the dunes, flooding the peats and burying the posts beneath the sea-borne sands. The North Sea, ever-restless, continued to wear and tear at the low-lying coast, stripping and washing away the layers of peat until 4,000 years later, in 1998, the posts surfaced once more.

Archaeologists are not entirely sure what the circle was for. One possibility is that it was constructed after the death of an important tribesperson. The dead body would have been placed on the flat surface of the central, up-turned tree stump. Birds and other scavengers would pick the bones clean. Eventually, the skeleton would be removed and taken for a final burial elsewhere.

When the press got hold of the story of the find and the dig, they quickly dubbed the timber circle 'Seahenge'. Like Stonehenge, the structure is circular and possibly had something to do with burying the dead, but that's where the similarities end. Seahenge is a wooden construction. It is relatively small in scale. It is a few centuries younger than its stone cousin.

These differences weren't enough to put off New Age pagans, including Rollo Maughfling, self-proclaimed Archdruid of Stonehenge and Glastonbury. The druids and pagans claimed that the 'henge' was theirs by spiritual right and that moving the timbers would destroy the circle's power and significance. They wanted the posts left where they were, on the beach. A number of local people also objected to the plan to excavate the 'henge' and remove it to a museum. It was good for tourism, they said.

However, the North Norfolk Coast is also an internationally recognised nature reserve, rich in birdlife. The naturalists were worried that increased visitor numbers would be bad for the birds and their breeding habits. The arguments between the pagans and the tourist industry on one side and the bird lovers and English Heritage on the other became increasingly fraught, fuelled in part by a gleeful press.

It was clear to the archaeologists that the exhumed wooden posts, now exposed to the air and the sea would soon be worn, washed, bored and eaten away. They were in no doubt that if the timber circle was to be saved, it would have to be excavated and preserved.

First they sought injunctions against the more forceful protesters. Then they began their dig. When the timbers emerged, they were taken to be washed and cleaned. In 2003, they were transferred to the Mary Rose Trust in Portsmouth where the slow, complex business of protecting the oak timbers began. Like the Tudor warship before them, the Bronze Age timbers were finally preserved and sealed in a special wax. Today, the re-constructed 'Seahenge' can be visited and seen not too far away at the Lynn Museum, King's Lynn.

Holme Beach, where the henge re-emerged, is just one stretch of the sandy fringe where Norfolk slopes passively into the sea. The county has wonderful beaches. Some are wide, low and sandy. Some are shallow, steep and pebbly. The vast majority of the pebbles are flint. But every now and again, if you are sharp-eyed and keen, you will see a pebble that isn't a grey-white flint. Some of these rarities are beautifully coloured, red and orange, pink and grey, or purple and blue. Today, I am on the look out for these pretty, hand-sized, far-travelled rocks.

I am back on the beach, walking west from Cromer. The morning mist has lifted and the sun is beginning to burn away the thin white cloud. The sea is in sleepy mood. Its lazy waves have just enough energy to tumble the smaller pebbles, to and fro. As the stones gently rattle and roll in the waves, they are slowly ground to silky smoothness. The fine-grained flints glisten white, iron-stained yellow, and grey. But of the rare few that are not flint, you can see crystals of dazzling white quartz and pink feldspar. In some of these pebbly exceptions you can trace the flow lines of once half molten rocks. But what on earth are these non-flinty, exotic pebbles doing on a beach in North Norfolk? The nearest outcrops of rocks that might once have given birth to these alien visitors are hundreds and hundreds of miles away, in the north of England, the Scottish Highlands and the mountains of Scandinavia.

Extraordinary detective work by generations of geologists, both professional and amateur, has gradually pieced together a remarkable story. There is a thrill as nature's power and the vast passages of time are sensed. Mighty forces must have been at play allowing me to hold one of these far-flung travellers in the palm of my hand. To understand their journey and how they got to the beaches of North Norfolk, we need to plunge once more back into the Ice Age.

In previous ice advances, as the climate began to shiver and more snow fell over the mountains of the north, the glaciers began their inexorable flow. Above them, frozen mountain peaks shattered in the extreme frosts. Rock fragments tumbled onto and into the ice. The glaciers became armed with scree. With their rocky cargo, they could now scour and scrape, chisel and gouge, file and flow their way down the valleys and slopes. And on they pushed, joining forces with other frozen rivers, to form massive ice sheets until eventually they slipped and slid across the plains and river basins, carrying their booty of rock and stone plundered from far and wide.

In time, though, as the climate warmed and the ice sheets melted, they gave up their rocky treasure. Their ground down and shattered plunder was dumped. Morraines formed. Veneers of clay, silt and sand were spread across Norfolk's chalky bedrock, ice-smoothed, wind blown and undulating. Melt waters tumbled pebbles into ice-dammed lakes and the rising sea. The itinerant rocks now found themselves set free and abandoned far from their home in the gravels of North Norfolk, on the beaches of Sheringham and Cromer, and the spits of Blakeney and Scolt. Most had hitched rides on the greatest of the Quaternary Ice Sheets, the 450,000 year old and fittingly named Anglian. We now call these alien pebbles of Caledonian granite, Highland gneisses and Scandinavian plutonics *erratics*, or even more formally, *allochthyonous rocks*. (See *Plate 21*) They are vastly outnumbered by the pebbles of flint that have been released locally from the underlying chalk by ice and water.

Perhaps the most distinctive, the most rare, and to my eye most beautiful of these very occasional, far travelled strangers is the polished, silvery blue-black rock known as *larvikite*. It is packed with shimmering, schillerising crystals of feldspar, bleached grey, white and light sandy brown by sun and sea. Larvikite is only found in Norway – near the town of Larvik south of Oslo.

Larvikite is an igneous rock. It formed from molten magma deep under the Earth's crust. There it cooled very slowly allowing big, glittering crystals of feldspar to grow. All of this took place nearly 300 million years ago beneath a new mountain range that was being pushed up along an ancient continental edge. The chain ran from what is now North West Ireland across the Central Highlands of Scotland over to Norway.

Over the hundreds of millions of years since, the mountains of North West Ireland, Scotland and Norway have been worn down by ice, wind and rain to reveal their igneous roots, including the Scandinavian rock we call larvikite. During the Quaternary Ice Ages, frost-shattered fragments of the larvikite peaks fell into the ice below. They were carried away, out across the frozen wastes of the North Sea Basin. When the ice sheets eventually melted, a few, just a precious few of these larvikite rocks found themselves dumped far from home, cast amongst the sands and boulder clays or tumbling along in the glacial meltwaters or left to roll in the waves of the deepening North

Sea. Given their far-away, long-ago, subterranean origins, it is extraordinary that every now and again, we might, just might, spot one of these small, rounded pebbles, fashioned from larvikite, lost amongst the flints of a Norfolk beach, 600 miles from their Scandinavian home.

A few weeks after my meeting with the West Runton mammoth, I was sitting a mile or two further east on the breakwater rocks beneath the cliffs at Sheringham. The huge, roughly cut, fridge sized boulders lay jumbled beneath the sea wall. They felt warm under the sun's glare. And as I looked down and around the rocky masses, I saw flashes of light and rainbows of colour as the crystals sparkled in the bright summer light. The feldspar crystals in the rock were showing off. They were displaying that glorious trick of schillerisation, the result of very fine layers within the crystals diffracting the light, like a film of oil on a pool of water or the flashing iridescence of a dragonfly's wing on a summer's day.

I was surrounded by thousands of tons of rock. And the rock was larvikite. My search earlier in the month for the rare ice age, ice borne, hand sized pebbles of the exotic rock had proved fruitless. I smiled. What had taken nature hundreds of thousands of years to do, men had done in a geological instant.

Like most North Norfolk coastal towns, Sheringham is under constant attack from the sea. Arctic gales and winter storms regularly drive ferocious waves against the fragile cliffs. Rising sea levels only make matters worse. The world's ice caps continue to melt as temperatures rise, naturally and by man-made global warming. Each year, billions of tons of water are added to the Earth's oceans. On top of which, the whole of southern Britain, see-saw-like, is ever-so gradually sinking while Scotland is slowly rising as it bounces back, now free of the massive weight of ice that depressed its mountains and glens as it lay under the Devensian Ice Sheets. All of which means that sea levels around the coasts of southern England and East Anglia are rising millimetre by millimetre, year on year.

Without protection the silty, boulder clay cliffs of Sheringham are easy prey to the clawing waves of the North Sea. In bad winters, the sea can claim many metres of any land left exposed, naked and without defences.

Sheringham town rests between two small hills. To the east is the Beeston Bump as denoted on OS maps or Beeston Hill as many Sheringhamians prefer to call it. And to the west is the higher Skelding Hill rising 170 feet above the beach and the sea. It is capped by an observation hut which was once a former coast guard station but is now a look-out post maintained by the local coastal watch group. Sloping off south and west of the hill are the greens of Sheringham Golf Club.

The town is protected from coastal erosion by a concrete sea wall which also serves as a promenade. To beef up these defences, 20,000 tons of Norwegian larvikite have been shipped across the North Sea and massed on the beach against the seawall. Each block of 'rock armour' as the Environment Agency calls them, weighs 8.5 tons.

So Sheringham is safe behind its walls of concrete and its rock defences. And even though I failed to find any Norwegian erratics, I am surrounded by thousands of tons of Scandinavian larvikite. The older blocks have weathered a pale sandy-white and pale grey, although the feldspar crystals still sparkle in the sunlight. Of course I am not alone in my love of the shimmering silvery blue rock. You can see it along any high street. It is the polished rock face of choice for many shops and banks, especially banks, inside and out. Café counters, pubs and bars all love it. In fact in 2008, so great was the petrological pride of Norwegians, they voted larvikite their national rock. Of course, they might be the only country in the world to have a national rock. Does the UK have one? If so, what could it possibly be?

Portland Stone? Aberdeen Granite? The Chalk Cliffs of Dover? Welsh slate? Yorkshire Coal?

As I was waiting to catch the morning train to Sheringham, I bought a cappuccino from the little coffee shop (now demolished) in the middle of the Norwich station concourse. The counter was a small but perfectly formed slab of polished larvikite. Keen to share my knowledge I casually mentioned to the barista that this pretty rock was from a small town in Norway, and wasn't it beautiful. 'It needs a lot of wiping and polishing,' replied the young woman, grumpily. 'People slopping their coffees all over the place.' And with that the conversation ended.

This proved to be my second larvikite rebuff. You'll have guessed by now that I have a fondness for the rock – its history of slow cooling deep beneath some ancient Scandinavian mountain chain hundreds of millions of years ago, the steady growth of thumb sized crystals of feldspar that scatter shards of brilliant light across the spectrum, its noble journey entombed in ice, its worthy voyage to defend our coasts as rock armour against raging seas. You get the idea. And you won't be surprised that when it came to choosing a new kitchen work surface, well, there was no contest. Larvikite it was and larvikite it had to be.

Again, keen to show off my expertise in matters of rock, I just happened to point out to the two big kitchen fitters that the heavy work surface they were heaving into place was made of a rock called larvikite – yes, all the way from Norway. And look at those scintillating crystals of feldspar. Isn't it splendid? The men of granite were unmoved.

'It's heavy, I'll say that,' said Ryan. 'We call it Blue Pearl because that's what it says in the catalogue. And we get it from York, where they store it and cut it. No one mentioned Norway. Now if you wouldn't mind just moving aside, sir, while we try to slide it into place.' The romance was entirely lost. And as I sat on Sheringham's sun-warmed sea defences, was there really much romance in these brutish blocks of rock armour compared to my search for a single, rare, far travelled, ice rafted pebble, polished by wave and ground by ice over thousands of years? The massive quarry blasted boulders, stacked on a Scandinavian quayside, had been shipped across the North Sea in a matter of days. And though fractured out of the same mountain mass, the sea-shipped journey of the Sheringham 'armour' stone could not compete with the pebbly poetry of frost-shattered mountain peaks, rivers of ice, and a journey of a million years.

Chapter 3
Mass and Energy

It was while I was reflecting on my failed search for a fist-sized, far-travelled, sea-smoothed, feldspar-rich pebble and feeling slightly dizzy thinking about mighty distances and the slow tick of the geological clock, who should be sitting behind me only a few feet away, with a mug of tea in his hand, was none other than that genius of deep time and big space, Albert Einstein.

As you stroll along Sheringham's promenade, the cliffs up to the town are shored by massive concrete walls. The walls keep the sea at bay and the cliffs in place. To brighten up the drab creamy white slabs, artists have painted pictures of dolphins and whales, fish and fishermen, sea gulls and geese, deckchairs and ice cream vans. Towards the western end of the promenade on the wall of a café is a painting of Einstein. He is sitting on a beach, holding a mug of tea. He stares straight at you with those twinkly eyes and his crazy white hair. (see *Plate 1*)

The image intrigues visitors, some of whom take photographs and post them on websites. The more cultured amongst them, upon first seeing the painting, believe they know why he's there. They say to themselves and their readers 'Ah, Einstein on the Beach! The artist must be a Philip Glass fan.'

In 1975, the American composer Philip Glass, in collaboration with the theatrical producer Robert Wilson, wrote a four-part opera, *Einstein on the Beach*. It premiered the following year at the Avignon Festival in France. The opera is five hours long, without breaks. The collaborators originally titled the work *Einstein on the Beach on Wall Street*, but somewhere along the way, they dropped 'Wall Street' for reasons that neither creator can now remember.

But there is another, much more fascinating explanation of why Einstein is pictured having a cup of tea, on a beach, along the sea front of a Norfolk seaside town that's nothing to do with Philip Glass and his opera.

Commander Oliver Locker-Lampson was a barrister and Tory Member of Parliament. He was a man who became opposed to all forms of totalitarianism, whether of the left or right, including German National Socialism. In 1933, he proposed a bill to extend British citizenship to Jewish refugees escaping Nazi persecution. Although the bill failed, he remained personally active in helping many Jews get out of Germany.

His family owned a summer home at Roughton, just south of Cromer, a few miles south east of Sheringham and not far from Beacon Hill.

In spite of Einstein's brilliance, it was increasingly obvious that 1930s' Germany was no longer a safe place for a Jew, genius or otherwise. His work was condemned by the Nazis as 'Jewish science' and 'scientific Dadaism'. So in September 1933, Einstein, who had already fled Germany for Belgium, was now helped by Oliver Locker-Lampson, to escape the growing dangers of mainland Europe.

The physicist managed to board ship for England and after stepping off at Dover with only a bag and battered violin case, Einstein was taken by Locker-Lampson to Norfolk. There, he was given temporary sanctuary in a number of small thatched wooden huts, one for his bedroom, one for a kitchen, and one, so the story goes, for a piano. The huts were built on the rough grass and scrubland of Roughton Heath, not far from the Commander's own home. The strange choice of accommodation was apparently for Einstein's safety. At the time, the location was a closely guarded secret and security was tight.

Einstein was only in Norfolk a few weeks. However there are several delightful black and white photographs including one of him standing in a field, patting the head of a small pony, ridden by Commander Locker-Lampson, accompanied by a

Miss Billing and her friend (both carrying rifles), and the local gamekeeper wearing a cloth cap, also there for the great man's protection (See also *Plate 2*).

We don't know too much about what Einstein did while he was staying in the area, whether he managed to do much work on his equations, or whether he ever sat on the beach at Sheringham drinking tea. But his brief stay on the heath, amongst the heather, protected by his two rifle-toting 'angels' seems to have been a quiet and happy one.

However, we do know that on 3 October he made a trip to London. He was asked to speak at a packed meeting held in the Albert Hall to raise money to help other endangered academics escape the Nazi regime in Germany. The event was chaired by a fellow Nobel prize-winning Cambridge physicist, Ernest Rutherford. Other speakers included Joseph Chamberlain, Maude Royden and William Beveridge.

Einstein warned of the dangers of imminent war. He spoke of the need to maintain our freedoms. 'If we want to resist the powers which threaten to suppress intellectual and individual freedom,' he said, 'we must keep clearly before us what is at stake, and what we owe to that freedom from which our ancestors have won for us after hard struggles.' The audience cheered.

Four days later, on the 7 October 1933, Einstein boarded the ocean liner *Westmoreland* at Southampton. It had set sail from Antwerp. Already on board were Einstein's wife, Elsa, and his loyal secretary, Helen Dukas. Ten days later they landed in New York. They were met by friends and supporters who drove them on to Princeton, New Jersey. Einstein never visited Europe again. He remained at Princeton University until his death in 1955, aged 76.

A contemporary of Einstein's was the sculptor Jacob Epstein. Although their life courses flowed in opposite directions – Epstein was born in New York but moved to London in 1905 – their paths crossed briefly in that Norfolk September of 1933.

Jacob Epstein visited Albert Einstein in his Roughton Heath hut on three occasions, each time for a sitting. He would have liked more but the authorities were keen to get Einstein on the boat for America. Although he was now in England, there were still fears that the scientist might be in danger from anti-semitic Fascists, hence his odd hideaway. Epstein's own parents were also Jewish refugees. They left Poland to settle in New York where, a few years later Jacob was born, a year after Einstein, in 1880.

Epstein stayed at the Royal Cromer Hotel, long since demolished. On three consecutive days, he visited Einstein in his crowded little hut. Each sitting lasted two hours, after which Einstein would smoke his pipe and play either the piano or his violin.

On several counts the meetings between the two men seem as unlikely as they were extraordinary. A hut on Roughton Heath near Cromer. Both men in their mid-fifties, both Jewish. A scientist and an artist. One a genius on the mathematics of geometry and time; the other gifted in the aesthetics of shape and form. One who understood space in the mathematical and abstract, the other who explored space by feel and touch. And out of their bizarre coincidence we have a rendering of Einstein that captures his essence in a small bronze bust, just 44.5 cm high. Talking of his subject, Epstein described his hair as wild, floating in the wind, but his look was 'a mixture of the humane, the humorous and the profound'.

Six castings were made of the bust. One is lodged with The Tate in London while others can be found in museums and galleries in various cities including Cambridge, Liverpool and Jerusalem.

The unlikeliness of someone as famous as Einstein living in a hut, in Norfolk, in 'cheerful exile' as he described it, has continued to fire the imagination. Epstein in clay and metal; Glass in music and sound. Glass, in turn, inspired the Californian rock band 'Counting Crows' who recorded their own 1994 version of *Einstein on the Beach* (I won't distress you with the lyrics). And then in 2004, the author and playwright, Mark Burgess, wrote *Einstein in Cromer*, a radio play that first aired in May of that year.

Admittedly rather convoluted, but no less rewarding, it is also possible to explore another link in which Einstein's genius and insights help make sense of Norfolk, its geology, character and current position on the face of the planet. It involves a bit of science, a lesson in bomb making, some violence, huge forces, and to my mind at least, a rather pleasing explanation of why the county has so many flint churches.

In 1905, Einstein published four papers that revolutionised modern physics and our understanding of space, time, mass and energy. Presented in one of those papers was this famous man's most famous equation: $E = mc^2$. In this 1905 paper, he showed that energy (E) and mass (m) are equivalent. You can convert one into the other. This was a profound insight and it had far reaching consequences.

Because the 'mass' side of the equation (m) has to be multiplied by the speed of light (c) *squared* (that is 300,000 kilometres per second *times* 300,000 kilometres per second, producing the enormous number 9,000,000,000,000 km/sec), it means that a very small amount of mass or matter can be converted into a huge amount of energy (E). His unravelling of the relationship between matter and energy led to all manner of explanations and understandings of the universe in which we live.

It turns out that there are two basic ways of producing enormous of amounts of energy from small quantities of mass. One is to fuse atoms together to make heavier elements. This is nuclear *fusion*. The other is to split the atoms of large, unstable, radioactive elements to create smaller, lighter elements. This is nuclear *fission*.

Nuclear fusion requires huge pressures and extremely high temperatures. This can be achieved at the centre of stars and it causes them to shine. In the process very small amounts of the combined masses of the fusing atoms are converted into prodigious amounts of energy. This is $E = mc^2$ at work. The energy released makes its way slowly through the star eventually to appear at the surface as light and heat which then radiate out into space. And so we *see* the sun and *feel* its heat, and life on Earth becomes possible.

So, starting with the simplest element, hydrogen, stellar nuclear fusion gradually creates heavier and heavier elements as atoms of increasing mass are forged together – helium, carbon, oxygen, iron, silicon, magnesium and sodium. Each fusion releases yet more energy. And so gradually in the unimaginably hot furnaces at the centre of stars, each one of the 92 naturally occurring elements can form in a process known as stellar nucleosynthesis – the creation of the elements in the womb of stars.

But eventually each star runs out of nuclear fuel. The bigger ones collapse and then explode in a violent, immensely energetic finale. This is a supernova. In their death throes, supernovae shine briefly but brilliantly, brighter than anything else in the night sky. And as they explode and rage against the dying of their night, they scatter their remains as dust throughout the cosmos, casting into space motes of carbon, oxygen, iron and all the other elements forged in their fiery hearts.

Over time and across space, some of this dust, under gravitational collapse, will be re-cycled to form new stars and the planets that condense around them. The thrill, as so often observed, is to know that we are stardust. Planet earth and all that lives and grows on it, made up of elements of oxygen and hydrogen, carbon and iron, and so many more of the natural elements, is stardust, the settled ash of long dead suns, reborn. As you look at your hand, feel the warmth of the fire, smell the flowers, it is beautiful to think that far away and long ago, each atom of your being was fashioned in some ancient star.

The heaviest elements, such as uranium and radium, are 'heavy' because they have the most dense nuclei, packed full of protons and neutrons. Some of the heaviest elements and their various isotopes are unstable. The protons and neutrons in their over-crowded nuclei find it difficult to live together. So over a set period of time – known as a half-life – half of any given mass of a radioactive element will break down into two, less heavy, more stable elements.

A particular isotope of Uranium, known as Uranium 235 is especially unstable. If it absorbs just one more neutron, its nucleus splits producing two lighter elements – barium and the gas krypton. This splitting of an unstable radioactive element is known as nuclear *fission*. In the fission process a number of sub-atomic particles including alpha particles and electrons escape with great energy and at high speed. Gamma rays are emitted. There is also a small loss of overall mass. It is during this breakdown process that the radioactive isotope releases vast amounts of energy.

So far, scientists and engineers, using unstable radioactive elements, have managed to create and control the processes of nuclear fission. We see it every day in nuclear power stations where the energy released in the form of heat, turns water into steam and the steam drives a turbine which produces electricity.

It was apparent from the beginning that producing power from nuclear fission was easier but much less efficient and more 'dirty' than generating energy from nuclear fusion. However, trying to mimic what stars do naturally and build nuclear power stations based on nuclear fusion is proving fiendishly difficult. The prize of success promises to be huge. Hydrogen from water offers an almost limitless supply of fusion's raw material. The process is relatively clean. And the energy released would be immense, meeting almost all of the world's needs.

More military-minded scientists also became interested in the processes of nuclear fusion, nuclear fission, and the sudden release of unimaginable bursts of energy. First they learned to make atomic bombs based on fission. Then with more devilish refinement they managed to create hydrogen, that is to say thermonuclear bombs based on fusion. It was atomic fission bombs that were dropped on Hiroshima and Nagasaki in 1945.

Five months before his death, Einstein said he regretted the indirect part he had played in the creation of nuclear weapons. 'I made one great mistake in my life,' he said, 'when I signed the letter to President Roosevelt recommending that atom bombs be made; but there was some justification – the danger that the Germans would make them first.'

In his final days, Einstein also co-signed the manifesto issued by the mathematician and philosopher, Bertrand Russell, encouraging fellow scientists to 'appraise the perils' of nuclear weapons, and for governments to acknowledge that 'their purpose can never be furthered by a world war, and we urge them, consequently, to find peaceful means for the settlement of all matters of dispute between them.'

The Russell-Einstein Manifesto, published in 1955, brought about the first of many Pugwash Conferences, so-named after the unlikely sounding town of Pugwash in Canada where the first conference took place. They represented the beginnings of campaigns for nuclear disarmament and nuclear test-ban treaties across the world. From his 1905 equation to his 1955 manifesto, Einstein remained committed to peace: 'Remember your humanity, and forget the rest,' he said.

Einstein's equation, $E = mc^2$, explains why nuclear fusion releases so much energy. The equation explains the origin of stars, the creation of the elements, and the dust of our being. Nuclear fission, the breakdown of unstable elements into lighter more stable atoms helps us to understand radioactivity. And it is radioactivity that helps explain why, along with the sands along the beaches, there are flints on the shore and chalk in the cliffs of Norfolk. Indeed, lying beneath most of Norfolk there are hundreds of metres of chalk, banded with nodules of grey-white flint. The fact that Einstein once happened to sit on an East Anglian beach, above a bedrock of chalk, surrounded by pebbles of flint was made possible because, as he had famously shown, energy and mass are equivalent. And the German for a stone? *Ein stein*.of course.

To explain how chalk forms, to puzzle over why so many of Norfolk's medieval churches are built of flint, and to wonder why we have spent some time talking about Einstein and thinking about radioactivity, we need to go on one more geological field trip.

Chapter 4
Chalk and Flint

It's late summer and I am taking an early morning train to Sheringham. The night has been muggy and we rumble through a still drowsy, sun-warmed countryside. As the train approaches the coast the track cuts through the leafy low hills of the ice-dumped debris that is now the Cromer Ridge. And an hour after leaving Norwich I arrive in Sheringham. But today I'm ignoring the town's rock defences, sea walls and picture of Einstein and taking the Coasthopper bus all the way to Hunstanton, a seaside resort tucked away in the far north-west of the county. The bus, as the name suggests, hops along the North Norfolk coast from Cromer to King's Lynn. Just under two hours later I'm standing on the beach, beneath the cliffs, at Hunstanton. I am looking at Norfolk's earliest and oldest deposits of chalk rock. They rise above the shallow waters of the Wash and look across the sea to Boston and the flat fens of Lincolnshire. (See *Plate 3*)

Although I am here in the morning, the best time to see the cliffs is when the sun is beginning to set. As the west facing cliffs beneath the town catch the glow of a summer's evening sun, the visitor is treated to an unusual but striking sight. A band of rich, sunlit, rust-brown rock is overlain by a thin layer of pink, brick-coloured chalk which in turn is capped by yet more chalk, but this time coloured a brilliant white. (See *Plate 4*) At first glance, the cliffs don't look quite real. The unlikely contrasts between the rusty browns, the reds and the pure white are stark. The cake-like layers of ginger browns and strawberry pinks look good enough to eat beneath the icing-sugar white of the cliff tops. It is approaching midday and I sit down on a rock amongst the pools and stare back at the cliffs, smiling as I always do at the improbable sight.

The rocks at Hunstanton were laid down at the beginning of the Cretaceous period, which began around 145 million years ago. Initially, the seas in which the sediments settled were close to land. However, around 110 million years ago, the geography began to change. The waters became turbulent and shallow. Coarse and pebbly sands were deposited. It is these rough sands that form today's ginger brown rocks at the base of the Hunstanton cliffs. They are known as the *Carstones* and can be found outcropping in quarries and riversides in a long, thin strip running north to south from Hunstanton to Downham Market before eventually disappearing beneath the Fens north of Cambridge.

These Lower Cretaceous carstones, although not the best rocks for the skills of the stonemason, are all that is locally available as a building material in many western strips of Norfolk. These rough iron-rich stones with their distinctive rusty, dark brown colour have been used to build houses, walls, pubs, and the occasional church. But in spite of their coarseness, they give houses a warm, distinctive look, the look of a gingerbread house.

The two lodge houses that guard the entrance to the Queen's royal estate at Sandringham offer pretty examples of these 'gingerbread' houses. There are a few 'gingerbread' churches too. St Mary's, for example, is a 13th century church, albeit much restored by the Victorians, built on the outskirts of Downham Market at Denver. This little church sets the rugged carstone against a fading white limestone to great effect. The only note of discord is sounded by the great historian of architecture, Nikolaus Pevsner who notes that the stain glass windows are the work of one Ian Pace, whose efforts, he observes are 'not common' before caustically adding 'which is a good thing.'

Above the carstones is the *Red Chalk*. Around 100 million years ago as the Cretaceous seas began to widen and deepen, the waters became calmer. The layer of Red Chalk in the Hunstanton cliffs reveals a gradual change in the ancient marine environment, one in which the red river clays could still wash gently out to sea and where the waters were quiet enough for these fine iron-rich sediments to mix with the white chalky remains of small, dead plankton. The result was a soft, limey ooze that gradually turned to rock beneath the weight and pressure of yet more chalky pink layers. This resulted in the red chalk we see today.

By the beginnings of the Late Cretaceous, just under 100 million years ago, the seas over what is now East Anglia were getting even wider and ever more deep. They were now free of the muds, silts and sands washed down by the far away Cretaceous rivers. All that rained down on the sea floor was a slow, steady drizzle of the dead skeletons of tiny planktonic algae known as foraminiferans and the even smaller coccoliths that bloomed in the sunny waters hundreds of metres above.

The tiny plates and remains of these small creatures were composed mainly of the white mineral, calcium carbonate. And so century after century, for the next 30 odd million years, the sea bed continued to sink beneath layer upon thin layer of the soft white calcareous ooze. In these warm, balmy seas, the rate of sea bed deposition was very, very slow. Every 1,000 years the ooze thickened by just one more centimetre.

With further downward movements of the earth's crust in this part of what is now north west Europe, the oozes compacted and hardened. They 'lithified' and turned into stone, the soft, pure, very white limestone which we know today as Chalk.

Chalk rock occurs in vast undulating sheets which rise and dip across north western and central Europe, from the Crimea, across the Paris Basin and fields of Belgium, and on to the white cliffs of Dover and the English Downs, over to Salisbury Plain, across to East Anglia, up to Yorkshire, and even crop up, now and again, in Northern Ireland and the Inner Hebrides.

The first person to suggest a name for these white rocks was the extravagantly named Belgian geologist Jean Baptiste-Julien D'Omalius d'Halloy, the only son of an ancient and noble family. In 1822, when describing and mapping the gently rolling landscape of the Paris Basin, he talked of the *terrain crétacé* – the chalky land. The Latin for chalk is *creta*, and hence the period in which these chalk rocks were deposited has become known as the Cretaceous.

Back in Norfolk, surveys and boreholes have shown that there is 1500 feet of chalk lying beneath the eastern half of the county. The oldest beds, including those we have already met in the cake-layered cliffs of Hunstanton, outcrop in the west. And from there, the whole formation dips gently east. This means that the top of these great chalk beds - the youngest - are to be found in the east. By the time we get to Great Yarmouth on the far eastern fringes of the county, the top of these same chalk beds has dipped so deep that the distinctive white rocks lie 500 feet beneath much younger marine sands and gravels, known as the Norwich Crag and the Wroxham Crag, which lie unconformably above the ancient soft, bright limestone. There is a 63 million year gap between the top of the Chalk and the Pliocene and Pleistocene Crags of Norfolk. The Crags are amongst the youngest of Britain's 4 billion year old geological history. They are at most a mere 2 million years old and were laid down on top of the old eroded chalk bedrock.

Chalk is a very porous rock. It can store rainwater for thousands of years. Farmers can dig wells and irrigate crops. Water authorities can tap the artesian pools and slake the growing thirsts of industry and town. And when the Chalk takes its gentle dive beneath the North Sea, its buckles and bends create the collecting sites for the oil and gases that have percolated upwards from the even deeper, slow-baked Carboniferous coal measure beds below. It can be used as a building stone known as 'clunch.' Indeed bright, white houses made of chalk can look stunningly attractive as any walk along the streets of Brancaster, for example, will reveal. However, as a rock, chalk, though useful for making lime, spreading on fields, and writing on blackboards, is generally too soft and crumbly to be used as a regular building material, but it does have a surprise up its sleeve.

While the calciferous and silaceous planktons were drifting in the ancient chalk seas, sponges were growing on the sea bed. Their skeletons were made of silica – silicon dioxide – the same mineral as quartz and sand. When the sponges died, the silica joined the limey ooze on the sea bottom.

Over the millennia, the silica from the sponges and the silaceous plankton dissolved into a gel as it sank deeper beneath the chalky sediments. It was then re-deposited in the gaps and holes left by worms and other creatures that had been burrowing on the sea bed. Some of the silica replaced the chalky minerals themselves. And as the silica gel filled these odd shaped holes and replaced the chalk it also lost its water. Tiny crystals of silica slowly turned into flint, brittle and hard.

Today, when you find flint *in situ*, you see it as bands of broken black and grey set in the bright white rock of the Chalk. The shapes it takes are irregular and nodular, the shapes of the sea bed burrows and holes where it dried and crystallised. It is Chalk, the softest of rocks, that has flint, the hardest of rocks, running through its veins. And when, nearly a 100 million years later, the flinty nodules wash out of the Chalk cliffs, they are rolled to and fro by wave and tide where they are gradually worn down into the smooth, rounded grey pebbles that crunch beneath your feet and make walking that bit more difficult as you plod along the shingle.

The point about these Late Cretaceous seas, in which plankton drifted and sponges grew, was that they were warm, wide and subtropical. As I stand on the beach today staring out across the greys and greens, purples and bronzes of the North Sea, it is clear that we are a long way from the tropics. So how can we explain the accumulation of so much warm-water life that helped create the hundreds of feet of the feta-white Chalk?

The whole late Cretaceous world 70, 80, 90 million years or so ago was a warmer place. It was a time of increased volcanic activity and high levels of greenhouse gases. There was naturally occurring global warming. Ice caps had long since melted and the oceans were 600 feet above their present-day levels.

It is actually quite difficult to imagine a world in which the margins of all the great continents were no longer land but shallow seas, teeming with life – plankton and sponges, shellfish and starfish, ammonites and belemnites, sharks and ichthyosaurs.

Moreover, the geography of these lands and seas was also very different from those we see today. Not only was Cretaceous Norfolk a warm, wide sub-tropical sea, *it was much further south than it is today*.

Today, Cromer lies nearly 53 degrees North. It sits on the same latitude as Labrador and northern Mongolia. However, 100 million years ago, Cromer was over 1000 miles further south, hovering around 40 degrees North of the Equator, the same latitude as modern-day Spain, southern Italy, the Mediterranean, and the Azores. Add together the effects of higher global temperatures *and* a position far to the south of today's chilly North Sea, you begin to understand why these seas of the Late Cretaceous were balmy and warm.

The explanation for Norfolk's, indeed the whole of Europe's northerly shift in global position is, of course, continental drift. The Earth's crust is made up of a number of giant plates which roam, slowly, over the surface of the planet. The process is known as plate tectonics.

The crust is made up of 15 of these major plates, seven primary and eight secondary. The primary plates underpin the ancient centres of most of the planet's great continents. So we have the African, Antarctic, Eurasian, Indo-Australian, North American, and South American Plates. The Pacific Plate, although it doesn't support a continent, is nevertheless a significant structure in the Earth's current crustal make-up.

The extraordinary thing is that these plates slowly, ever-so slowly shunt around the surface of the planet, sometimes crashing into each other, one diving beneath the other creating great mountain chains such as the Himalayas and Alps. Or sometimes the diving, colliding plates create deep ocean trenches, new islands, volcanoes, and yet more mountains as well as violent earthquakes. This is the lot of Japan and the islands of Indonesia. Sometimes two plates slide and scrape by each other, generating earthquakes and massive fault lines in the rock. As the Pacific Plate slides north and the North American Plate slips south, the San Andreas Fault appears as a mighty tear across the Californian landscape.

And sometimes plates pull apart. Once upon a time the North American and European Plates were joined as one. However, about 170 million years ago, they began to rift and go their separate ways and as they did, the Atlantic Ocean began to open between them. In the gap, new oceanic crust appeared as molten lavas plumed upwards and solidified between the splitting plates. Today this split and its associated lava eruptions appears as the mid-Atlantic Ridge which occasionally breaks the ocean's surface as a volcanic island – Iceland, the Azores, and St. Helena. The two continents are still going their separate ways at a stately speed of 4 to 5 centimetres a year. In another one hundred years, New York will be 5 metres further away from London.

For a long time, geologists and other earth scientists puzzled over the origins of mountains and the formation of the oceans. Initial explanations favoured the idea that the Earth's fiery birth billions of years ago meant that it was once very hot but has been cooling down, very slowly, ever since. The interior of the Earth is still hot enough to explain why the temperature rises as you go down a deep mine, and why hot waters and molten lavas occasionally erupt at the surface.

The argument went that if the Earth was once hotter than it is now, and it is gradually cooling down, then like all cooling things it will be slowly shrinking. As it cools and contracts, the rocks on the crust's surface will wrinkle and crumple forming great mountain chains and deep ocean basins.

This explanation invited the question: 'If this is the case, then how old is the Earth?' Geologists studying the thousands of metres of sedimentary rocks and the huge variety of evolving fossils found in them were beginning to think that the Earth needed to be millions and millions of years old if their observations were to make sense. The evolutionary biologists, including Charles Darwin, were also beginning to think about how much time they would need to make sense of the appearance of new species, and like the geologists, they were also talking about hundreds of millions of years. All of this was a far cry from the calculation that had been made by the very reverend James Ussher.

Ussher was the Archbishop of Armagh in Ireland. In 1650, based on a very careful reading of the biblical Book of Genesis, the Archbishop worked out that the Earth was created on Sunday 23 October 4004 BC. Yes, he was that precise.

The idea that the Earth was a mere 6,000 years old seemed ludicrous to 19th century geologists and biologists. So they decided to try and estimate the age of the Earth scientifically rather than theologically. If, they argued, the planet is slowly cooling from its molten beginnings, then knowing the rate of heat loss and the current condition of the Earth, it should be possible to calculate the age of the planet.

One of the key figures to have a go at this sum was another Irishman, William Thomson, who later became Lord Kelvin, a title he took from the River Kelvin, a northern tributary of the lower Clyde which flowed not far from his laboratories at the University of Glasgow. Born in Belfast in 1824, he went on to study at the University of Cambridge before spending the rest of his academic career in Glasgow. He enjoyed extraordinary success as a mathematician, physicist and engineer.

Perhaps he is best known for being the first person to work out the value of absolute zero, the temperature at which, put simply, atoms no longer transmit any thermal energy and, save for the weird effects of quantum mechanics, all internal motion ceases. It is not possible for temperatures to get any lower than this absolute point.

The value of absolute zero calculated by Kelvin, which has been revised only slightly over the years, was minus 273 degrees Celsius. In honour of his work, all temperatures which work from Absolute zero as their base are talked about in terms of degrees Kelvin ($^\circ$K). The freezing point of water on this scale, therefore, is approximately $+273^\circ$ K.

Given his expertise in matters of heat and temperature, Kelvin was drawn into the debate about the age of the Earth. After several stabs and many qualifications about the melting point of rocks and the state of the earth's interior, in 1897 he eventually estimated that the planet must be between 20 and 40 million years old. The geologists and biologists thought this figure was still far too small. For their processes to take place, they needed the Earth to be much, much older. A non-too friendly debate followed.

When the debate was at its fiercest, Kelvin was well into his seventies. By now he was famous, distinguished and few cared to disagree with him. If his calculations said the earth was only 40 million years old, then the geologists were wrong and they would have to re-think their ideas.

But it was Kelvin's fate to end his final days during one of science's most exciting times. In 1896, Henri Becquerel had discovered radioactivity in uranium. By 1898, Marie and Pierre Curie had added radium and polonium to the list of elements that were radioactive. And as they decayed, these radioactive elements emitted various sub-atomic particles and electromagnetic radiations, and, as we learned in the previous chapter, they released huge amounts of heat and energy in the process.

It soon dawned on geologists that this was a powerful way to explain where the Earth gets a lot of its internal heat from. If the radioactive minerals deep inside the earth, of which there would be vast amounts, were decaying and generating heat, this would explain how the planet was able to sustain high temperatures over millions of years. If at least half of the earth's internal heat comes from radioactive decay, the age of the planet could be increased significantly.

Modern-day calculations give an age for the earth of about 4.6 billion years, more than a hundred times older than the venerable Lord Kelvin's date based on the idea that the once very hot planet is slowly cooling. The new calculation meant that there was more than enough time to explain rock formation, rock deformation, fossils, and evolution.

Kelvin died in 1907, two years after Einstein established the equivalence of mass and energy in his $E = mc^2$ equation, the equation that would go on to help explain the huge amounts of energy released during nuclear fusion, star formation, the creation of the elements, nuclear fission, hydrogen bombs, and some of the heat produced by radioactive decay in the Earth's mantle that helps keep its interior molten and hot.

We're almost there in our quest to connect Norfolk's chalky cliffs and its brittle flints with our meeting with Einstein on Sheringham's seafront, nuclear fission and radioactivity. Just one final scientific breakthrough to tackle, one of global proportions.

Radioactive decay takes place throughout the planet, from the deepest levels of the Earth's core and mantle to the granite outcrops of Dartmoor and Aberdeen. When the heat generated by this decay is generated deep inside the Earth, temperatures become hot enough to melt rock. But because these rocks are buried beneath hundreds of miles of planet above, they are also under tremendous pressure. This means that although they are very hot, they can't fully melt so they behave more like a hot, sluggish, viscous plastic than a free flowing molten lava.

Between the base of the earth's solid crust and the planet's outer core, is a layer, thousands of miles thick, known as the mantle. The top of the mantle, just beneath the crust, has temperatures ranging between 500°C and a 1,000°C. However, the lower reaches of the mantle can exceed 4,000°C. This heat difference sets up mighty, slow moving convection currents.

When water is heated in a pan, the lower layers warm first and as a result their density decreases. With their lower density, the bottom layers begin to rise to the surface. Once at the surface, this warmer water cools slightly, becomes a little more dense, and once more sinks to the bottom, only to be reheated and sent in upward motion all over again. This cycle of heating and cooling sets up convection currents in the pan of water.

In exactly the same way, but on a much grander scale, huge, slow-motion convection cells are generated in the Earth's molten, plastic mantle. As the tops of these cells flow slowly beneath the Earth's solid surface, they drag the major crustal plates along with them. When two convection cells converge, cool and descend, the plates riding above them collide causing the crust to rise and buckle. The result is a mountain chain. When the rising currents of two cells fan out and flow in opposite directions, the plates being dragged above them are torn apart. Where they separate, great rifts and ridges form, and oceans open up.

The whole process of massive blocks of crust being dragged this way and that is known as *plate tectonics*. Huge slabs of the crust appear to drift slowly across the earth's surface, constantly re-configuring the continents and re-arranging the geography of the planet. I was first introduced to the idea of drifting continents when I was a student in the mid-1960s. The very idea of whole continents and massive blocks of crust being shunted around the Earth's surface, carried along on a churning mantle of hot, viscous rock seemed as wonderful as it was outrageous. But it explained so much. It explained mountains and oceanic trenches, earthquakes and volcanoes, warm water fossils being chipped out of today's cool temperate hills.

Forty years later after my first encounter with plate tectonics I was having lunch in the Sainsbury Centre at the University of East Anglia in Norwich. I had been invited by a retired maths professor to have a chat. He had read a book of mine about which he had a particular interest. But just as we were sitting down, he waved to an elderly, tall, bespectacled man who was carrying his tray of food looking for a table. 'You don't mind if a good friend of mine joins us?' asked Norman. 'No, of course, not at all.'

And so introductions were made. 'David, this is Fred, Fred Vine. Fred, this is David Howe. We're having a chat about one of David's books.' Well, I was speechless. Fred Vine. He was one of the geophysicists – a key player - who helped prove the reality of plate tectonics. He had spent much of his professional career at the University of East Anglia where he was now an Emeritus Professor. In the early 1960s, Frederick Vine had shown that ocean sea beds spread out on either side of mid-ocean ridges where the continents split, rift and separate. And as they do, so the oceans widen. Vine along with his colleague Drummond Matthews, and independently the Canadian Lawrence Morley, took advantage of the magnetic properties of cooling magmas and the regular switches of polarity that occur in the Earth's magnetic field over time. If the oceans are spreading out on either side of the mid-oceanic ridges as two plates pull apart, then the solidified lavas that well up through the crustal tear between the two plates should show symmetrical, bar-code like stripes of north-south, south-north magnetisation on either side of the ridges. And indeed, this is what they found. For example, from the late Cretaceous, as North America drifted away from Europe, the Atlantic Ocean steadily widened. The new oceanic rocks on either side of the Mid-Atlantic Ridge are the solidified remains of the lavas that constantly rise and erupt beneath the crustal rift, from Iceland in the north to Tristan da Cunha in the south.

I'm not sure that Fred, or indeed Norman, appreciated how excited I felt at this unexpected encounter. Not wanting to appear too smitten, I might just, you know, have casually mentioned to Fred that I knew of his early work on plate tectonics and left it at that. So here I was, forty years later having lunch with a kindly professor of mathematics and a distinguished geophysicist, someone who helped us to understand the Earth's dynamic nature and deep restlessness. Over the aeons, oceans come and go. Mountains rise and are worn down by ice, wind and rain. Seas appear but then get filled as rivers bring their muds, silts and sands to a final rest. The mortal remains of trillions of algae and plankton rain steadily down across the marine plains. Continents merge only to split apart and move off in different directions, centimetre by centimetre, year by year.

Geologists have worked out that over the last 500 million years, most (except North West Scotland) of the area we now call the British Isles along with the rest of Europe, has been on a slow, steady journey from roughly 50 to 60 degrees *south* of the equator to its present 50 to 60 degrees *north* of the equator. At different times, Britain has been a deepening sea, a filling-up sea, a shallow sea, a drying up sea, a mountain range, a desert, a tropical forest, a river delta, a land of volcanoes, and a land of ice and snow.

All this can be seen in the wonderfully varied geology of our Island: granites that were once the deep roots of rising mountain chains, basalt lavas that flowed across the unstable margins of advancing plates, red sandstones that were once deserts, yellow and orange sandstones that accumulated in river estuaries and sinking seas, the coals that were once tropical forests, grey-blue slates that began life as muds and oozes on the beds of ancient, deep oceans. And of course the limestones and chalks of those warm, tropical Cretaceous seas of long, long ago.

It is the sheer variety and complexity of the rocks found in these islands which in part explains why so many of geology's founding figures were British. The late 18th and 19th centuries saw the rise of many of the science's pioneers, especially in Scotland: James Hutton, a Scottish naturalist, often described as the founding father of modern geology; William Smith, William Buckland; Adam Sedgwick; the great Charles Lyell; Roderick Murchison; and the fossil collector, the remarkable Mary Anning of Lyme Regis, the discoverer of the first ichthyosaur, the first British pterodactyl and the first complete plesiosaur.

William Smith, born 1769, was a surveyor and the son of an Oxfordshire blacksmith. He was one of the first people to work out the correct sequence in which rock strata were laid down between the Cambrian, 542 million years ago, and the end of the Tertiary, 3 million years ago. In 1815 he published the first geological map of England, Wales and southern Scotland. Measuring a magnificent 2.6 metres by 1.6 metres it is still a thing of wonder and surprising beauty. The Natural History Museum in London holds five of the original copies as well as a replica copy on display.

Smith realised that the wide-ranging outcrops of chalk, including those of Norfolk, came somewhere near the top of his 'stratigraphical' sequence, and in a geological sense were therefore quite young, a mere 65-100 million years old.

However, what none of these geological pioneers appreciated, indeed could not appreciate, was how restlessly mobile is the Earth's crust. It was all very well describing the characteristics of the chalk, but it was very difficult to explain what a tropically formed, limey pelagic, marine sediment was doing this far north beneath the rolling downs and flinty fields of southern and eastern England. The full story could only be worked out when all the scientific pieces were eventually brought together, and this is how it goes.

According to radioactive dating, the Earth is 4.6 billion years old. Much of its past and present internal heat comes from the decay of uranium bearing minerals and other radioactive elements. These radioactive elements decay into lighter, more stable elements in the process known as nuclear fission that we met in the previous chapter. And, according to Einstein's famous equation, in these processes, as well as the production of an array of extraordinarily fast moving sub-atomic particles, small amounts of matter become converted into enormous releases of energy. All of these processes generate prodigious amounts of heat. This heat keeps the rocks of the mantle hot, viscous and 'plastic'. It also sets up the great convection cells which drag the surface plates of the Earth's crust this way and that across the planet in a never ending dance of continental rift and drift, fracture and collision. And as the continents glide here and there, so oceans come and oceans go.

One hundred million years ago, somewhere in the sub-tropics of the northern hemisphere, a sea, known as the Tethys Ocean lay between the great plates of ancient Africa and Eurasia. It was warm, several hundred metres deep, silt free, and teeming with life, including calcareous and silaceous plankton. Over the next 35 million years, the remains of this rich pelagic life fell to the sinking sea floor to form a lime-rich and silica-saturated ooze destined to become the Chalk with its bands of flint.

The African plate also continued on its grand journey north and as it did, the Tethys Ocean narrowed. Eventually, Africa bulldozed its way into the southern flanks of the European plate and the sediments of the Tethys Ocean. This slow motion inter-continental crash pushed up the Alps. It also compressed, tilted, buckled and bent the hundreds of metres of chalky muds that lay to the north of the newly emerging mountain chain.

Today we recognise these vast deposits of lightly crumpled lithified lime as the Chalk. The gentle rise and fall of these massive beds shape the Champagne Plains of northern France, the Downs of southern England, the White Cliffs of Dover, the

Needles of the Isle of Wight, the Chilterns, Flamborough Head, and the flinty character of Norfolk.

So the pioneering geologists and the paradigm breaking evolutionists were right; the Earth *is* very old. Lord Kelvin, in spite of his undoubted brilliance as a physicist, was wrong. Wrong, not because his actual calculations were in error, but wrong because he was unable, maybe unwilling to enter the vast time frames of the earth and life scientists, and because he did not know, indeed could not know all the thermodynamical variables that had to be taken into account when working out the age of the Earth.

Lord Kelvin did not live long enough to understand the significance of radioactive decay for understanding the Earth and its history. And although as a physicist he would no doubt have marvelled at the genius of Einstein's 1905 equations and revelled in the implications of radioactivity, they came too late for him to change his mind and see the error of his calculating ways. Another reason, perhaps, why Einstein, on the beach, by the chalk, amongst the pebbly flints, on the wall, at Sheringham, has a slight twinkle in his eye.

Chapter 5
Rights and Wrongs

Kelvin was in error. He made a mistake. However, one of the reasons that science has proved so successful and powerful is that it has a rigorous methodology that allows it to recognise and learn from its mistakes. One of the most original and intriguing essays on the presence and pursuit of error was written by Sir Thomas Browne, a practising medical physician. He was born in London's Cheapside on 19 October 1605, but he spent most of his professional life as a doctor in Norwich, Norfolk. He moved to the city in 1637 and died, on his seventy seventh birthday, 19 October 1682.

Exactly three hundred years after his birth, on 19 October 1905, the city of Norwich unveiled a bronze statue of Sir Thomas Browne, sculpted by Henry Pegram. Browne sits on a chair looking at a burial urn which he is holding in one hand while he rests his head against the other. (See *Plate 5*) The statue sits on Hay Hill adjacent to St Peter Mancroft church where the good doctor is buried, and just a few yards from the house in the Haymarket where Browne had lived and practised. The house has long since vanished and made way for new shops and walkways. However, a circular slate plaque on the corner of the Haymarket and Orford Place, affixed to the wall between two high-street shops, *Pret a Manger* and *Thornton's (The Art of the Chocolatier)* records that:

> SirThomas Browne
> Physician and Author of Religio Medici
> 1605-1682
> Lived in a house that once stood near this plaque
> At the junction of Haymarket and
> Orford Place

It's late morning and the city is busy and bustling. I find a spot where the flow of people is a little slower. And as I look at Sir Thomas's plaque the shoppers look at me. Most give me a passing glance but one or two cast their eyes to read what I'm reading. 'Do you know, I've never noticed that sign stuck up there,' says an elderly woman, smiling. 'I've heard of him but never noticed.' 'That's him, Sir Thomas Browne, over there,' I reply pointing towards his statue. 'Really? That's him? Sitting there? Fancy that. Most interesting. I've walked up and down here a hundred times and never taken any notice. You live and learn, don't you. I shall have to tell my husband. He likes that kind of thing. Thank you. Well I never.' And off she walks, still smiling, carrying her shopping, stopping for a second to take one last look at Sir Thomas on his high plinth silhouetted against the pale blue sky.

I look back at the plaque. I can't help thinking that Browne would have had fun with the siting of his commemoration, between a place that sells eats and one that sells treats, one for sustaining life and one for encouraging pleasure, a sandwich and a chocolate. His free-wheeling mind, a mind that saw connections and unlikely conjunctions of time and place everywhere, would certainly have smiled as he contemplated the plaque's location.

As well as being a busy doctor, Browne had interests in botany, anatomy, antiquarianism, religious debates, and literary discourse. He was curious about everything. He was a great collector of things – bird eggs, medals, books, plants, indeed interesting objects of every kind.

He saw himself, if not as a true scientist, then at least as someone who believed that science was the way to find the truth of things and eliminate error. Browne valued observation, experiment, gathering facts, and finding order. Collections and sets of particular things allowed him to look for patterns, see connections, detect likenesses. He saw each bit of the world as part of some greater whole and although there might be many pieces missing, he believed it was the job of thinking men and women to seek explanations that were plausible and consistent with observation.

In 1646 Thomas Browne published *Pseudodoxia Epidemica*, also referred to as *Vulgar Errors*, or even more fully *Enquiries into very many received tenets and commonly presumed truths which when examined prove but vulgar and common errors*. As most 17th century professional men were well-versed in the classics, his title derives from the Greek: *pseudo* (false) *doxia* (opinions) *epi* (something laid on) *demos* (people) – false ideas put about amongst the people, or simply, *Vulgar Errors*.

So successful was the book, it was a best seller in its day, running into six editions, each being revised in light of the latest scientific and historical findings. The book is extraordinary. Browne wished to challenge many of the commonly held facts, beliefs and superstitions of his day. When he believed they were wrong, these were his common or 'vulgar' errors.

He examined and analysed beliefs, both right and wrong, about plants and animals, electricity and magnetism, geography and history, minerals and stars. It is impossible to capture the sheer diversity and exuberance, quirkiness and even humour of Browne's interests and challenges. Here is a tiny sample of some of the subjects he addressed: dolphins, how to preserve a lodestone, can a lodestone cure gout, do men weigh more when they are asleep, nutmeg, phoenixes, poisonous animals, the colour of plants, Pliny's character, the sun, the causes of thunder, griffins, the purpose of the elephant's trunk, the toxicity or otherwise of elderberries, Adam's navel, and the story of a woman who got pregnant from taking a bath causing Browne to remark wryly that this must be 'a new and unseconded way in History to fornicate at a distance'.

It is fair to suggest that Browne was not an original scientist. He didn't conduct experiments, he didn't test hypotheses. He studied what others had said, discovered, claimed and believed in order to bring their views to a wider audience. He brought a scientific attitude to everything that he considered, collected and wanted to challenge. In this sense, he was a science populariser.

But he was more than this. He believed that science advanced through debate, discussion and disagreement. For him, dogma was inimical to good science. He thought that claims to being right, based on who you are and your authority, is not how science progresses. Our understanding advances as we explore and try to fit together the fractured world of our piecemeal knowledge. Conjecture and confrontation, co-operation and the discussion of possibilities are the way forward. And good heavens, doesn't Thomas Browne entertain a wonderful world of possibilities.

Whatever his subject, Sir Thomas offers his readers a bewildering range of approaches, any number of answers, a variety of interpretations, and all kinds of possible explanations. He considered how it was possible to see an object or a specimen first this way and then that, each leading to a different conclusion. Observation on its own, he believed, leads easily to false understandings – those vulgar errors. What is on the surface rarely reveals the underlying nature of things. We must keep open our options and ponder all possible explanations. He sought to clean up other people's messy and erroneous thoughts, leaving the scientific house slightly tidier and easier to manage.

But having rehearsed each belief and explanation, usually without bias, he didn't always reach a definite conclusion. He left the door open for different interpretations, alternative explanations. And as he went on *his* intellectual wanderings, he was helped on his way by taking note of what natural philosophers, historians, theologians, archaeologists, travellers, anthropologists, and antiquarians had to say.

The result is a book of marvellous, but peculiar variety. His musings triggered one line of thought, then another. His freely associating mind produced essays that were encyclopaedic, cabinets of curiosities in written form.

And equally impressive, Browne's need to capture the essence of an idea or a thing, coupled with a classical education encouraged him to coin scores of new words, dozens of which we still use today without giving a moment's thought to their original author. I'm still on Haymarket. I cross the street and sit down on one of the several polished black stone seats scattered beneath Sir Thomas's statue on Hay Hill. Each stone celebrates one of Browne's written works. I quietly mutter a few of the doctor's newly coined words which I read from one of his biographies. My mutterings, though, aren't as quiet as I thought. I earn more strange looks from the shoppers who walk by. Here are just a few of Browne's alleged neologisms that I whisper:

> ambidextrous, approximate, antediluvian, carnivorous, computer, electricity, ferocious, gymnastic, hallucination, holocaust, individual, incontrovertible, insecurity, literary, locomotion, medical, prairie, precarious, precocious, therapeutic, suicide, ultimate.

Browne's love of language also extended to an appreciation of the Norfolk dialect. In his own book about Norfolk dialects, Keith Skipper mentions Browne's tract *Of Language and particularly of the Saxon Tongue* in which the physician gives twenty six examples of 'words of no general reception in England but of common use in Norfolk.' Examples include 'bunny' – a bruise of swelling, and 'mawther' – a young girl or woman.

So although Browne may not be seen as a scientist of the first rank, he receives high praise for his writing, his prose, his style, his fluency. In his untethered attitude to writing and reflection, scope and expression, the Norwich doctor is not unlike the French essayist, Michel de Montaigne who died thirteen years before Browne was born. And in his turn, Browne has influenced others. His style, in which one train of thought leads to another, has been infectious. His structure and prose have been admired by writers as varied as Samuel Johnson, Charles Lamb, Virginia Woolf, Jorge Luis Borges, and W. G. Sebald.

W. G. Sebald was known as 'Max' to his friends and colleagues. He was born in 1944 in the small town of Wertach in southern Bavaria, part of the German Alps, sixty five years after Einstein was born and sixty five miles south of the city of Ulm, Einstein's birthplace.

After taking a degree in German literature at the University of Fribourg Sebald spent three years at the University of Manchester and a year in Switzerland before taking up an appointment as a lecturer in modern European languages at the University of East Anglia, Norwich in 1970.

To read Sebald can be a strange experience. His books are not novels in any conventional sense. They are part memoir, part traveller's tales. They are biographies which offer oblique reflections on life, times, places and events. Fact and fiction blur. Sebald himself sometimes described his writing as 'documentary fiction.' His words hypnotise; everything feels slightly distant, diffuse, elliptical, haunting. There is a feeling of disorientation, sadness, of floating slightly outside time.

Poor quality, low resolution, greyish photographs – snapshots, old press cuttings, paintings – appear throughout the text, adding to the ghostly, shadowy atmosphere as Sebald wanders and reflects through time and place.

He was an inveterate walker. East Anglia in particular, with its infinite horizons and sense of isolation, lent itself to his ruminative state of mind. From his home just outside Norwich he would take the train from the city's station to one of the many small, rural platforms dotted across Norfolk and Suffolk.

The second chapter of his book *The Rings of Saturn* begins with the author catching the be-grimed, sooty diesel train from

Norwich to Lowestoft on a grey, overcast day in August 1992. The railway line runs over flat, low lying fields and boggy woodland alongside the River Yare before it makes a crossing at Reedham Ferry. The line trundles its way over the marshes, by New Cut, until it meets the River Waveney. A few miles downstream, the Waveney joins the river Yare at Breydon Water, and together the conjoined rivers flow through Great Yarmouth and out into the North Sea.

Sebald gets off the train at Haddiscoe Station, the halt for Somerleyton Hall. He finds the platform deserted. To his left is 'the seemingly endless expanse of the marshes…There was not a soul about…' And so he begins his long walk through Suffolk, with its evocations, meditations, and reflections on 'the transience of all things human.'

The book actually begins and ends with Sebald reflecting on the life and works of Sir Thomas Browne. Both writers ponder life's arbitrariness and finitude. One thought leads to another reflecting the interconnectedness of things. Seemingly disparate and random events, people and places, past and present become linked, and one thing leads to another. 'I have kept asking myself,' ponders Sebald in another of his books, *Campo Santo*, '…what the invisible connections that determine our lives are; and how the threads run…' Life appears unpredictable. Individual stories cross, engage, change, and then move on. Reading and listening allow what was imagined in the past to seep into what we imagine today. It is when Browne's writing is especially elevated that Sebald feels uplifted, borne aloft on circles of 'spiralling prose' even as both writers meditate on the brevity of life as little more than a passing moment between two seas of eternal darkness.

My latter days working at the University of East Anglia were spent in The Elizabeth Fry Building, named after the Norwich born, early 19th century prison reformer. We moved into the new block in 1997. However, for the previous twenty one years, I had enjoyed an office on the top floor of one of the University's original, Denys Lasdun designed buildings overlooking the main car park and central walkway. There was a common entrance and set of steps into the building. Each of the five floors was occupied by a different School including those of English and American Studies, and European Modern Languages, the School in which Max Sebald taught for so long.

Over the years, those of who worked in the different Sectors and Schools learned to recognise one another, not always by name or School, but at least our faces became familiar. We might nod and smile in recognition as we climbed the steps, entered the lift or passed on the stairs. And this is where I first met W. G. Sebald. He was distinctive, handsome. He looked every inch the central European intellectual. We never really spoke, merely exchanging slight bows of the head by way of greeting. I didn't know who he was, and he didn't know who I was, other than we were both academics who worked in the same building.

That is until the year 2000. Like other universities, it was UEA's custom to award honorary doctorates to people who had distinguished themselves in a particular field. Every year each School would nominate an individual for the award. The celebrated individuals would receive their doctorates as part of congregation, the annual ceremony in which undergraduates collected their bachelor degrees and post-graduates their Masters and PhDs.

In 2000, Professor Sir Michael Rutter, the eminent child psychiatrist, had been nominated by my School. The School of English and American Studies was honouring the novelist Martin Amis. It so happened that these two honorary graduates were to receive their doctorates at the same ceremony. As a build up to the award's presentation, Schools would appoint an Orator. Dressed in heavy, colourful robes, he or she would deliver a five minute speech saying nice things about how splendid and worthy was their nominee. The congregation would then clap enthusiastically and the University's Chancellor or Vice-Chancellor would award the honorary doctorate.

I was to be the Orator for Professor Sir Michael Rutter. And as a fellow author, Max Sebald was to do the honours for Martin Amis. Before we processed to join the congregation we assembled in The Council House - the honorary graduates, the orators and other university officials. It was while we were waiting that I exchanged my only ever words with Max Sebald.

'Hot in these robes.'

'Yes, very.'

'Would you mind passing me that bottle of water. Thanks.'

'Is that your fellow?'

'Yes. Michael Rutter, a child psychiatrist. That's him over there talking to the Registrar. And you're doing Martin Amis?'

'Yes. He's slipped outside to have a cigarette. His second so far I think.'

'Ah, yes, I can see him. He looks a bit restless. We better call him in. It's time to get into line and process.'

'Good idea.'

The congregation went smoothly. The undergraduates and post-graduates received their degrees. Lots of clapping. Hundreds of smiling mums and dads. I gave my oration and Michael Rutter gave a gracious response, as is the custom. Max gave his speech and Martin Amis responded. I don't remember the details but I do remember he made a few ambivalent remarks about his equally famous novelist father, Sir Kingsley, whom he said was a mixed blessing, at least in terms of Martin developing his own writing career.

After the congregation I had to confess that I didn't actually know who Max Sebald was, other than a fellow academic in another School of study. I certainly I had no idea that he was increasingly being seen as one of the late 20th century's more important writers. When I learned of my ignorance, I set about reading his haunting work, becoming lost in his opalescent prose, and experiencing the feelings of floating and distance that his writing conjures. And it was reading *Rings of Saturn* and the influence that Sir Thomas Browne's writings had on Sebald that further spurred my own efforts wandering through Norfolk over place and across time.

Max, then, was a walking man. *The Rings of Saturn*, based on his Suffolk walks, was first published in German in 1995, and then translated into English three years later. By the time I was reading his books, my School's move to The Elizabeth Fry building had already taken place. My route to work rarely took me past my old office and I never saw Max Sebald again. He died in a car crash in December 2001, aged 57. The coroner's report said he had suffered an aneurysm.

Chapter 6
Walkers and Wonderers

I don't know whether Norfolk is unusual in its habit of producing writers who walk. Or indeed whether walking prompts some people to write and that Norfolk is a place made for walking. Whatever, the county has a good record – I was going to say track record – of being and becoming home to writers who walk and walkers who write. For example, in 2003, the inimitable Bill Bryson, author of books on travel, language and science, moved to live for a while in the old rectory at Wramplingham, seven miles west of Norwich. His book, *At Home: A Short History of Private Life*, is based on a tour of the rooms of his own house which was built in 1851.

Two hundred years before Bill's house move, on the 5 July 1803, the prodigious walker, linguist and adventurer George Borrow was born in his maternal grandfather's house in Dumpling Green near the market town of East Dereham, ten miles north west of Wramplingham.

Whether or not the poet William Cowper was a walking man I don't know. But his poor mental health accounted for him being a restless soul. In 1795 he moved to Norfolk with his companion, nurse, and carer, Mary Unwin. On first arriving in the county they stayed at North Tuddenham, then shifted to Swaffham, and on to Mundlesley for the sea air (which turned out not to suit), before finally settling in 1775 in East Dereham, Borrow's birth place. Not long after this last move, Mary died, casting the poet once more into a deep depression. In 1800, three years before George Borrow's birth, William Cowper died, aged 68. Browne, Borrow, Cowper, Sebald; Norfolk based and writers all. 'God moves in a mysterious way,' penned Cowper, 'His wonders to perform.'

An unhappy childhood was the lot of another of East Dereham's writing sons, a traveller in time if not on foot. Brian Aldiss, the science fiction writer, was born in the town in 1925. Aged only six, he was sent away to boarding school where he endured many miserable years. In later life, Aldiss became friends with Kingsley Amis, father of Martin. At the time, both men were heavy and dedicated drinkers. In a note to Aldiss, written in 1970, Amis advised 'Keep on with the good work, Aldiss, and don't get too sodding literary and you'll have put us all in your debt.'

George Borrow also boasted of his drinking prowess. At six foot three inches, he was a tall, imposing man. Dressed in black, sombrero on head, he cut an impressive figure as he rode and strode his way across the counties of Britain and the countries of Europe. In his poem, *Lines to Six-Foot Three Borrow*, he says of himself:

> A lad, who twenty tongues can talk,
> And sixty miles a day can walk;
> Drink at a draught a pint of rum,
> And then be neither sick or dumb;
> Can tune a song, and make a verse,
> And deeds of Northern kings rehearse:
> Who never will forsake his friend,
> While he his bony fist can bend;
> And, though averse to brawl and strife,
> Will fight a Dutchman with a knife.

Borrow's life was agitated and colourful. His father, Thomas, was a sergeant, later promoted to captain in the West Norfolk Militia. His mother was a tenant farmer's daughter. She enjoyed amateur dramatics and played minor roles with a company from the Theatre Royal in Norwich. It was while playing a small part in a production visiting Dereham that she met and married Thomas Borrow. Being an 'army' family, the Borrows moved a great deal but would periodically return to Norfolk.

George's father finally retired after fighting with Wellington at the Battle of Waterloo. The family settled in a house on Willow Lane, Norwich. On two separate occasions, George was a pupil at Norwich Grammar School, but he was prone to truant, for which he would be thrashed by the headmaster, Dr Edward Volpey.

In 1819, Borrow was articled as a clerk to a firm of solicitors in Norwich, Simpson and Rackham. However, the sedentary life of a legal clerk was no life for the young George. When his articles ended, he headed off to London where he tried his hand at writing.

Fact and fiction are not always easy to distinguish in George Borrow's accounts of his own life. He generally cast himself as hero in whatever he wrote. But he was certainly a gifted linguist. By the time he was a young man, he already knew several languages, including Romany. It was this talent that eventually encouraged him to apply for a job working for the Bible Society based in London, translating the Bible into other languages. It was 1832 and at the time he was staying in Norwich. He had little money. And so began one of his many extraordinary walks. He planned to march to the capital for his job interview.

Norwich to London is 112 miles. In 1600, it took Will Kemp nine days to walk from one city to the other. He was an actor, jester and friend of William Shakespeare. He had played Falstaff to much acclaim. However, he was not happy when the Bard turned him down for the role of the clown in Hamlet.

So, as a self-promotional stunt, he decided to morris dance his way from the capital to Norwich. With stops, rests, impromptu performances and general showmanship, the trip actually took him 23 days but in his write-up of the adventure he called the story *Kemp's Nine Daies Wonder: Performed in a daunce from London to Norwich (Containing the pleasure, paines and kinde entertainement of William Kemp)*. Upon arrival at the city via St Stephens Gate, he reports that: '…one Thomas Gilbert in name of all the rest of the citizens gave me friendly and exceeding kind welcome.'

Today in Chapelfield Garden just a few hundred yards from St Stephens Gate, there is a hefty eight foot tree trunk carved with a relief of Will Kemp morris dancing his way into the city. Mark Goldsworthy is the artist. In February 2011, Tom Clare, a pizza delivery driver from Brackley, Northamptonshire and a morris dancer, repeated Kemp's journey with beard, bells and hat, raising money for charity. And the city's Theatre Royal has named its restaurant 'Kemp's' in honour of the actor and marathon morris man.

George Borrow was a well-practised, long-distance walker. Nine days? Huh. Borrow claimed to have completed the walk from Norwich to London in 27 hours, with little rest, helped on his way only by a pint of ale, a half pint of milk, a roll of bread, and two apples. On arrival in London and after a brief interview, The Bible Society offered him the job. He was sent to Russia where he was involved in translating The New Testament into Manchu.

George Borrow suffered what today might be diagnosed as bi-polar disorder. He called his depressions 'the horrors.' Like many others before and after him, he walked as therapy. Walking was something he had always done. He was a wanderer by nature, and his wanderings both encouraged and were encouraged by his remarkable talent for languages. By his middle years, he had more than a working knowledge of Danish, Anglo-Saxon, Norse, Spanish, Russian, Hebrew, Gaelic, Greek, Latin, Arabic and allegedly many other languages. These skills certainly kept him employed as a translator whenever the need for money arose.

He was nearly 40 before he began writing about his travels, walks and adventures – in Spain, Portugal, France, Morocco, Ireland, Wales, Scotland, England…and Norwich where, as a schoolboy, he first met and revelled in the company of the Gypsies camped on Mousehold Heath, a stretch of high wooded ground on the northern fringes of the city. His traveller's tales are full of exotic encounters, extraordinary meetings, nights in pubs, and unlikely adventures.

His first major success as a writer was *The Bible in Spain*, published in 1843. The book was based on his five years in Spain working for The Bible Society. During his travels he met and made a study of Spain's Gypsies, learning their language and dialect in the process. This was followed a few years later by *Lavengro* published in 1851, with the subtitle *The Scholar, the Gypsy, the Priest*. The book is semi-autobiographical telling the story of young George Borrow, who takes to the road, has many adventures, and meets a gallery of rogues, priests, gypsies, prize fighters, horse dealers, damsels, and fairground folk. *The Romany Rye*, published in 1857, continues his rollicking story and further travels throughout England.

> On I went on my journey, traversing England from west to east - ascending and descending hills – crossing rivers by bridge and ferry - and passing over extensive plains. What a beautiful country is England! People run abroad to see beautiful countries, and leave their own behind unknown, unnoticed – their own the most beautiful! And then, again, what a country for adventures! Especially to those who travel on foot, or on horseback. People run abroad in quest of adventures and traverse Spain and Portugal on mule or on horseback; whereas there are ten times more adventures to be met with in England…Witness the number of adventures narrated in the present book – a book entirely devoted to England. Why, there is not a chapter which is not full of adventures, with the exception of the present one, and this is not yet terminated.

After his wife, Mary, died in 1869, Borrow lost much of his zest for life. He eventually returned to East Anglia where he spent his final days living in a house near Oulton Broad, Lowestoft. Age and infirmity meant he could hardly walk to the garden gate. He died in 1881, aged 78.

Perhaps the most enduring of George Borrow's books is *Wild Wales,* based on his extensive walks and wanderings in Wales in 1854. Published in 1862, many regard it as one of literature's best travel books. It certainly inspired the travel writer, naturalist, biographer and poet, Edward Thomas, himself a compulsive walker and whose mind was also prone to be troubled and unsettled.

Many of Thomas's essays, books and poems were about his walks in the countryside. *Beautiful Wales,* published in 1905, was a book written by Thomas and wonderfully illustrated by the painter Robert Fowler. Thomas had read Borrow's *Wild Wales.* He makes reference to the adventurer's 'epithets' as Thomas himself travels, describes and reflects on the land of his Welsh parents' birth. His admiration of Borrow is sealed a few years later in a biography of his fellow depressive and wanderer. *George Borrow: The Man and His Books* appeared in 1912. 'Borrow,' wrote Thomas, 'could touch nothing without transmuting it' later adding:

> Borrow came near to being the perfect traveller. For he was, on the one hand, a man whose individuality was carved in clear bold lines, who had a manner and a set of opinions as remarkable as his appearance...[and] he had abounding curiosity. (p 174)

Although there is no record of Thomas taking extensive walks in Norfolk, his book, *The Icknield Way,* does begin – just - in the county. Thomas opens with a beautiful chapter on roads, ways and footpaths – as routes, metaphors, as ways to escape, as ways to get home. The Icknield Way is that ancient road that wanders through East Anglia, over the Chilterns, and south to the Downs of Berkshire and Wiltshire before dropping to the sea in Dorset. At its northern tip, it begins where the Peddar's Way ends, on the very southern fringes of Norfolk, just east of Thetford. From there, it heads south into Suffolk.

Although on modern maps the Icknield Way looks like a continuous, purposeful pathway, originally it was probably a series of shorter Neolithic walkways, some dating as far back as 6,000 years, running roughly from Norfolk to Dorset. Over time, as people were searching for more direct and efficient ways to move up and down the country, and as walking enthusiasts were keen to explore the romance of ancient roads, the Icknield Way took on a more coherent, connected character.

Edward Thomas therefore began his 1911 walk of the Icknield Way at its northern end near Thetford, 'a most pleasant ancient town, built of flints, full of turns and corners and yards.' As well as describing what he saw and the people he encountered, Thomas reflects on life's meaning and his own, often troubled state of mind. And it was Thomas's walks along the Icknield Way that inspired Robert Macfarlane, Cambridge Fellow in English, walker, environmentalist, and travel writer, to describe his own 'journey on foot' in his remarkable book *The Old Ways*.

Macfarlane left his home in Cambridge to begin his walks with the 'ghost' of Edward Thomas urging him along. Chalk makes for good walking country. It is porous; the rainwater percolates quickly away. Its ridges are open, rounded and smooth. Its crests afford the walker clear views of the way ahead, the destination to be reached, and in ancient times, dangers that might lurk. Macfarlane heads south but if we walk north and east back into Norfolk, the chalk landscape becomes more subdued. The repeated advance and retreat of the ice sheets has planed the hills, covering them in a veneer of sands, silts and boulder clays.

These recent, unconsolidated Ice Age sands and clays are best seen along the Norfolk coast where they form the soft, crumbling cliffs between Happisburgh and Overstrand, round the shoulder of Norfolk and the town of Cromer and west to Sheringham. It is these cliffs, particularly when exposed and unprotected, that the rain and sea wear away, sometimes metres at a time when the tides are high and the weather stormy. As well as occasionally revealing the bones of mammoths and the antlers of deer, the erosion releases millions of tons of sand, refreshing the beaches and creating the dunes.

As you continue west from Sheringham, the North Norfolk coast suddenly changes character. Standing as I am now on top of Skelding Hill, to my east are the undulating, retreating cliffs that head off towards Cromer. Looking west, towards Blakeney, the land is low, flat and salty. Between the villages of Weybourne and Blakeney, Wells-next-the Sea and the Burnhams, Brancaster and Holme next the Sea, the coast is one of creaks and mudflats, saltmarsh havens and sandy spits. Blakeney Point is one such sensuous spit of shingle and sand.

A few years before his Thomas-inspired walks along *The Old Ways*, Robert Macfarlane took himself off to the wild places of Britain – mountain tops, remote valleys, wind swept moors, dark forests. No Sunday stroller with a soft bed and a hotel dinner waiting at the end of a long day, Macfarlane would shelter for the night in a bivouac bag on a Scottish peak or nestle on a moor in a cradle of heather and grass beneath the stars.

One hot summer's afternoon, he arrived at Blakeney and walked out onto the Point. He crunched along the flint pebble beach. The sea was to his right and the sandy spit and dunes to his left. It is four miles to where the Point curls and cusps towards the land and where the waters of the Blakeney Channel and Blakeney Pit wander sinuously out into the North Sea.

After a bathe in a tidal pool by the wooden hull of an old sunken boat, and clearly made of sterner stuff than most of us,

Robert reached the Point's western tip, opened his sleeping bag, and settled for the night in a sandy hollow between two dunes. The evening was full of sounds – of ducks and geese flying home to roost, of honking seals beaching themselves ready for sleep, of the 'chatter' of dingy lanyards clanking in the breeze.

He awoke at six the next morning, with a pain in his back from a night on the sands. He retraced his tracks off the Point, recovered his car and drove south to Suffolk to visit his friend and kindred spirit, Roger Deakin. Roger was a fellow writer, fellow tree-climber, naturalist, environmentalist, film maker, and author of *Waterlog: A Swimmer's Journey Through Britain*, an account of his wild swims in rivers, lakes, lochs, ponds, dykes, moats, canals, tarns, rock pools, seas, spas, lidos, and, yes, swimming pools too. *Waterlog* became an introduction, guide and inspiration for all wild swimmers to take the plunge and get a 'frog's eye view' of the country. Not long after Robert's visit, Roger became unwell, dying a few months later in August 2006 of a brain tumour.

As his literary executor, one of Robert's achievements was to collect Roger's many boxes, writings, notes and papers and arrange, with the help of Professor Jon Cook, to have them archived at the University of East Anglia. The remarkably varied and eclectic collection now constitute the Roger Deakin Archive, housed in the University's library. Amongst the archive's treasures is the pair of Speedo trunks in which Roger wild swam his way through Britain.

No doubt Roger was wearing these trunks when, on a June evening in 1996, he slipped into the deepening waters of the Stiffkey Freshes. The Freshes are a network of tidal creeks and shallows that take shape where the River Stiffkey joins the Blakeney Harbour channels as they round Blakeney Point and flow into the North Sea. He records that he saw a deep pink moon rise over the sands and shingle that make up the Point. The tide was rising, fast as it does around these parts. It raced silently over the muddy sands.

And while he was drifting happily on the incoming tide, Roger remembers Henry Williamson's descriptions of swimming here with his children. Williamson was the author of many books but most famously *Tarka the Otter,* first published in 1927. In 1936 Williamson bought a farm in Stiffkey. This venture encouraged him to write *The Story of a Norfolk Farm* published in 1941. However, after a difficult few years and a failing marriage, Henry Williamson gave up his farm and returned to Devon, the county and its rivers that had inspired his story of the life of Tarka the otter.

Stiffkey in the 1930s appears to have been something of a risky place for professional men. Harold Francis Davison was the son of a preacher man. After a jolly time indulging in amateur dramatics, he followed in his father's footsteps and trained to be a priest. He was ordained in 1903. A few years later, H. F. Davison (M.A. Oxon) was posted as rector to the parish of Stiffkey. He was a popular vicar. With the poorest of his flock, he was generous with both his time and money. He served in the Great War as a naval chaplain but on his return was upset to find that the dates of his wife's pregnancy did not exactly align with his own periods of home leave.

Now quite how this affected his mind, we don't know. What we do know is that he began to visit London, ostensibly to save the souls of the capital's fallen women, the city's street prostitutes. Although his good works did not bother his more humble parishioners overly much, Norfolk's gentry were less happy with their vicar's Christian zeal. A scandal ensued. It captured the nation's imagination. Newspaper headlines such as 'Randy Rector of Stiffkey' and his own description of himself as 'The Prostitutes' Padre' did not help his case.

Outraged Stiffkey gentlefolk and investigations by the Bishop of Norwich were determined to see the vicar's redemptive interests as more than spiritual. But in spite of largely uncorroborated, mainly circumstantial evidence, a London-based church trial held in 1932 found him guilty of immoral conduct. He was, as seems apt given the accusation, de-frocked and stripped of his holy orders, no longer a priest.

Penniless and homeless, if he didn't exactly run away to the circus, he did the next best thing and found himself on Blackpool's seafront, in a barrel, entertaining, performing, and sermonising. He was hoping to raise money to campaign for his innocence. But disillusioned with Blackpool's vulgarity, in 1937 he joined Fred Rye and his animal-themed seaside show in Skegness.

In the middle of one of his acts which involved being in a cage, Davison managed to upset Freddie, his fellow performer. Freddie was a lion. Freddie, feeling rather agitated, bit Harold's neck and shook him violently. The attack was fatal and two days later, the late Vicar of Stiffkey also became the late Harold Francis Davison. Although the act was billed as 'Daniel in a modern lion's den', on this occasion, sad to say, Davison's career as a lion tamer was short lived.

It is October. The day has been still beneath unbroken low grey cloud. I end my walk gazing across the muddy greens, dusty yellows and glossy browns of Stiffkey Marshes watching the tide steal its way back amongst the creeks. Unlike Roger Deacon, I am not tempted to take a swim but I do remember the Reverend Davison's sad, fleetingly notorious life as the Prostitute's Padre, a failed lion tamer and one time Rector of Stiffkey.

Chapter 7
Sand and Sea

Perhaps Roger' Deakin's watery inspiration was still drifting around the Stiffkey Freshes and Blakeney Point ten years later when Robert Macfarlane found himself in the sun-warmed pool by the sunken hull taking a late summer dip. Even as Robert was leaving Blakeney and long before he arrived in Suffolk to visit Roger, the sea breezes had destroyed all traces of his sandy bedtime hollow. This is a restless place. If the eastern fringes of Norfolk are forever being lost and re-worked by high seas and rising tides, the spits and marshes of Blakeney and Brancaster find the coast in more creative mood. Norfolk is a county where destruction and construction play endlessly across the landscape. As the tides and currents drift west, so the cliff washed sands of the eroding east settle, flow and shift their fingery way past Cley and Wells and beyond to Scolt Head and Holme.

As the Edinburgh to Norwich flight begins its descent along the North Norfolk coast, and if the skies are clear, your eye is drawn to the flowing beauty of this fractal, in-between world, where land and water caress and curl. From five thousand feet up, the sandy fronds wave yellow and bright against the dark sea. (See *Plate 6*)

But this is also a fragile place. There are no cliffs here. Barely above the level of the purple-grey sea, strong winds and storm surges threaten to breach the dunes and drown the marshes whenever the tides are high and the air pressure low. Geomorphologists call it a dynamic coast. The re-curved spits and dunes, channels and creeks re-form and re-assemble every day, subtly, sneakily, occasionally with violence, sometimes with great destruction.

The southern edge of this low, mile wide, salt marsh coastal strip runs in a relatively straight line from Weybourne in the east to Holme next the Sea in the west. As you approach the edge of this saltmarsh fringe, the land rises gently up the glacial tills and boulder clays that hide the chalk beneath. Geologists speculate that this ruler-straight east-west line between the saltmarshes and glacial hills marks the course of an old buried channel that formed when the last Ice Sheet reached its southern limit, stood still for a while and allowed vigorous rivers and freezing waters to flow directly east along its base where they carved a long, straight, neat valley groove before flooding out across the plains of Doggerland.

Further speculation wonders whether this line also represents a deeper, even more ancient fracture in the chalky bedrock below. As the great African plate began its slow-motion collision with Europe, some 40 to 50 million years ago the Alps crumpled into being. The northernmost ripples of this planetary crash zone, although less severe, pushed the Cretaceous rocks of southern England, northern France, Belgium and the Netherlands into gentle folds and broad basins. The Weald, the Downs, and the eastern tilt of the Norfolk Chalk are all the result of this southerly nudge by the African plate. And when the pushes and strains became too much, the rocks slipped and slid, broke and faulted.

So, possibly, just maybe, think the men and women of The British Geological Survey, the neat line dividing the salty marshes and the stormy spits from the rising clays and fertile ridges is the healing scar of an old crustal wound, a palimpsest in which the modern landscape continues to overwrite the older stories recorded in the rocks below.

As you move from sea to land, the character of this low-barrier coastal strip changes. Storm-beach shingle of rounded flint pebbles, spits, islands, vast sandy flats which at low tide disappear into the far-away sea, and marram-grassed dunes give way to a more sheltered zone of salt-marshes and tidal flats. At low tide, the creeks are empty and smooth-mudded.

They glisten, sensuous, muscled and glossy brown. As the tide rises, the creeks flood with surprising speed. Small rivers snake their way across this land-sea world, bringing with them fresh muds and silts, helping the marshes keep pace with the rising sea levels.

When Christine Abel first settled in this magical place back in 1968, she was struck by the contrast with her own native Devon. 'Instead of roaring Atlantic rollers breaking against high Devon cliffs,' she writes, 'there was a new alien sea that sneaked furtively up the creeks through expanses of marsh and followed me across beaches in flurries of small murky ripples at a remorseless walking speed that seemed slightly menacing.' I like 'sneaked furtively' and 'slightly menacing.' Almost before you realise, the sea that wasn't there a minute ago is suddenly everywhere, all around, across the sands, flooding the now brimful creeks. Many a time I have sat and watched fascinated by this daily ebb and flow, land slipping into sea and back again. It is dreamy and I find it mesmerising. And with similar thoughts, Patrick Barkham, the natural history writer, revisiting Scolt Head, describes North Norfolk's subtle charms as they seep into you 'like the trickle of the incoming tide…soothing and strangely uncompromising.'

Whether it's a quality of the light, the endless sands, the sense of vast space and emptiness, or the way sea and sky dissolve, this part of the coast feels different, mystical, not quite of this world. Most travel writers describe feeling lost, small, wonderful, insignificant, thrillingly meaningless, or ecstatic whenever the landscape or the elements overpower their senses. The Romantics experienced these feelings of the sublime whenever they had contact with untamed nature and beauty in the raw. Wild winds and thunderous storms excite. Raging seas mesmerise. Rugged mountain peaks remind you how very small you are in such a very big world.

However, you can also feel it in places where the world seems to have no edges, no beginnings, no ends. Holkham Beach is one such place. (See *Plate 7*) At low tide it forms a vast, flat sandscape that disappears without distinction into sea and sky. It lies between Wells-next-the-Sea to the east and Burnham Overy to the west. For Roger Deakin it was a place of peace and healing. It was where he would go whenever he felt sad. He would feel himself cross 'into another land, another state of mind'. He would experience a 'sudden lightness of being' and time would pass more slowly. Under huge skies, he felt nothing more than a dot on the horizon.

It is November and I have taken the Coasthopper bus from Sheringham. I get off at the stop outside the Victoria Hotel at Holkham and walk down Lady Anne's Drive. There are no cars parked here this early in the morning. I carry on, over the boardwalks, through the pine trees and arrive on the sands. This is my favourite time of the year to be on Holkham beach. The sky is a pearly, nacreous grey-white and I can't tell where the sea ends and the sky begins. The chilled air is opalescent and still. There is no sound. It is absolutely quiet. And there is no one else but me in this boundless, eerily silent world. The elements fuse. Sand-sea-sky. And in this formless place, my self feels as if it too might dissolve and de-materialise. I seem to be all things and no thing, everywhere and nowhere, in the moment and out-of-time in a universe that is entirely indifferent to my existence. The feeling thrills and unnerves in equal measure.

Suddenly, the spell is broken. Materialising out of the soft white light, two race horses gallop by. With flaring nostrils and steamy breath condensing in the cold morning air, they head across the wide sands for the sea. Splashes of white flash as the horses run through the salt waters. Sea horses.

Riders bring their stallions and mares to the beach to relax, train and get well. The grandest sight is when, once a year, the Household Cavalry bring their horses and riders to Holkham.

They escape London and their ceremonial duties for a few days of uninhibited running along the sands. The horses trot in the sea. Equine thalassotherapy. On this late autumn day, the muffled quiet returns as suddenly as it was broken as the two women and their horses canter off and disappear towards Wells-next-the-Sea a mile to the east. I follow their direction. It's only a short walk between the dunes, by the pines, beneath the beach huts along the sands to Wells.

Wells-next-the-Sea is unusual in the world of sea ports. It is a port, albeit a very small one, without a river, set back a mile inland from the sea shore. Boats can only sail in and out during a two hour window at high tide. Nevertheless, Wells takes boats of up to 750 tons and a ten foot draft.

The small town sits on the southern edge of the saltmarshes. A tidal channel, known as The Run, weaves its way towards The Pool and eventually into Wells harbour. The twice daily tide scours the channel of silt, which along with periodic dredging, keeps it deep enough at high water for boats to sail in and out from the open sea.

There has been a port at Wells for 600 years and probably much longer. In the 18th century the town was exporting wool and cloth. The trade was profitable and inspired the townsfolk to name one of their inns *The Golden Fleece*, a public house that still does business today. The pub is one of the places where the Commissioners for Havens and Creeks, first appointed in 1568, continue to hold their meetings.

By the middle of the 19th century, Wells was enjoying around a thousand ship movements a year in and out of the port. Cargoes of wheat, barley, malt, flour and locally fished oysters were exported. And ships laden with timber, coal, salt, rape, linseed, and building stone would unload their goods to meet local needs.

But the age of steam age left no part of the country untouched. It was the arrival of the railway in 1857 that marked the beginning of the end of Wells as a thriving port. Trade by sea gradually declined. There was a brief revival between the 20th century's two world wars as barley, malt and sugar beets were shipped out, while coal and potash were sailed in, but the fillip was temporary.

The nearest mainland European country to Norfolk is the Netherlands, 120 miles due east, only a bit further than Norwich to London. There has always been a lot of trade and traffic between the county and its continental neighbour. The Dutch registered North Sea sailing clipper, ALBATROS, was built in 1899 as a cargo ship. (See *Plate 8*) She remained a regular and faithful visitor to the port of Wells until 1996 when she unloaded her final commercial cargo of Belgium soya beans. However, don't be deceived by these humble duties as a commercial carrier of grain. During the second world war, ALBATROS smuggled Jews and dissidents out of Nazi-occupied Denmark. On her return visits, laden with goods, she hid guns and explosives destined for the Danish Resistance.

ALBATROS was a ship of the North Sea and the Baltic, cutting the waters between Norway and Scotland, Germany and Sweden, Belgium and Poland, Finland and Denmark, Norfolk and the Netherlands. In 2001, she returned to Wells. She was now working for Greenpeace as a 'sailing classroom' before earning her keep as part of The Albatros Project which was finally dissolved in 2005. ALBATROS made her last commercial sailing in 2008, freighted not with grain but paying guests.

Today Wells remains a busy place. It is a holiday town with cafes, shops and cottage-lets. Its harbour and moorings are full of dinghies and sailing boats, the occasional commercial ship, and pleasure craft which take you to see the seals, birds and spits. However, there is one old lady moored on the quayside whose sea-faring days are over, except for her three yearly sail to Yarmouth and back to renew her certificate of seaworthiness.

The old clipper, well past her hundredth birthday, still looks splendid, though on a summer's evening when the sun is low, you might just detect a blush of embarrassment across her black and white bows, for the ALBATROS is now a bar and restaurant. But true to her adventurous past, she is a restaurant with character, a bar with distinction. The food is Dutch, the ale is real, and the reviews excellent. I recommend the pancakes. But on this autumn day, I arrive too early for lunch and instead take the bus back to Blakeney.

Blakeney lies just a few miles east of Wells. It too was a commercial seaport until the beginning of the 20th century. But unlike Wells, the tidal scouring is less robust and gradual silting of the channels now means that only small boats can navigate their way from the sea to the harbour quayside. The silting of the channels and river mouths is a familiar process along this stretch of the coast. However, it wasn't always the case.

Throughout medieval times, many of the coast's winding channels led to small, but nevertheless sheltered and deep-water harbours, at least at high tide. And because the ports were typically set a mile back from the open sea, the names of the town reflect their geography. So no 'on-the-sea' or 'by-the sea' here. Instead, we have Wells-next-the-sea, Cley next the Sea, and Holme next the Sea, some with hyphens and some without. But with rising sea levels and lower river gradients, the fight to keep the channels deep, open and silt free became a losing one.

In their natural state, the saltmarshes hold enormous amounts of water. Twice a day the tides flush in and out. The marshes act as stops and filters for the sand, silt and mud that flow down in the rivers and in from the sea. It was these low tidal marshlands that proved too great a temptation for the county's 17th century landowners.

Keen to increase their estates, and insensitive to local trades and traditions, the big estate holders began to build embankments to claim land from the sea. As predicted and feared by the local sailors and fishermen, the man-made embankments upset the flow of both rivers and tides. The scouring of the channels that had kept the villages of Cley, Wiveton and Blakeney as prosperous ports since medieval times ground to a halt. The once navigable River Glaven which had enjoyed unhindered exit into the North Sea began to silt up. The little ports of Cley on the east bank and Wiveton on the west could no longer take sea-going boats. No more fish were landed on their quaysides; no more cargoes were unloaded at the ports.

Today, as the Glaven reaches the coast, it takes a sharp turn left and becomes the Cley Channel before joining the Blakeney Channel. Then, after several detours, it eventually finds its way out to sea. Cley and Wiveton, once thriving ports of medieval Norfolk, now spend their days as quiet rural villages.

There are several villains in this piece. In 1522, Sir John Heydon was the first to have a go at building banks to keep out the sea. A century later, while the Dutch engineer, Cornelius Vermuyden, was busy draining the Fens, another Dutchman, Jan van Hasedunch, made further improvements to Sir John's initial efforts. Then Simon Britiff, Lord of the Manor, decided to add another bank on the eastern side of the river Glaven. And finally, in the 1640s, Sir Henry Calthorp, completed the job of holding back the tidal waters.

The salty creeks of Cley and Salthouse became freshwater marshes. Ironically, the embankments and attempts at drainage were never a great success. The intended pastures and grazing land failed to become a happy home for the sheep that were planned to make the gentry's fortune.

Even more ironic, nearly four hundred years later, what was bad news for the 17th century sailors and fisherfolk of Cley, Salthouse and Blakeney turned out to be good news for their modern day descendents. The marshes – the Fresh Marshes of Blakeney, Cley Marshes and the Salthouse Marshes – are internationally important wildlife habitats for all kinds of bird life. The busy and sometimes exotic wild life attracts visitors throughout the year.

Many of these coastal marshes – both salt and freshwater – are now nature reserves. The oldest of the reserves are the Cley Marshes. An enthusiastic birdwatcher, Dr Sydney Long, bought the land in the 1920s for £5,100 to safeguard its character as a bird breeding and bird resting sanctuary. In 1926, he established the Norfolk Wildlife Trust, and Cley Marshes became its first reserve. Further west is Titchwell Marsh run by the Royal Society for the Protection of Birds. And the purchase of Blakeney Point and its transfer to the National Trust as a Nature Reserve in 1912 also gave Blakeney a new lease of life.

The whole of this sea-born, sea-sculpted, sea-threatened land is now part of the Norfolk Coast of Outstanding Natural Beauty. It stretches from the Wash in the west to the sand dunes of Winterton in the far east. The storm shingled spits, the windblown dunes, the salty creeks, the tidal marshes, the freshwater ponds and lagoons conjure a world of strange beauty. Little wonder that it attracts sightseers, walkers, bird watchers, artists, naturalists, weekend sailors, and second-home owners keen to escape city life.

For the last thirty five years, Mark Cocker, naturalist and environmental activist, has made Norfolk his home. He writes regular pieces for *The Guardian* newspaper's Country Diary. This is Mark wonderfully capturing the faded beauty of the saltmarshes around Morston, Holme and Cley. The saltmarshes, he writes:

> ...create the matrix in which the whole thing sits; they bind it all together and give it both wildness and authenticity. Created over decades in silt layers by the high tide, saltmarsh is as niggardly a landscape as its name connotes. There's no primary colour, contour, built-structure – except the odd wrecked ship with

its rotting vestige of human story – and no trees. The tallest plants are the salt-loving bushes called shrubby seablite. Along with the other dominant species such as sea purslane, the seablite is so quietly green it's only just this side of that chromatic boundary that marks out the living from the dead.

However, as we have seen, the coast is under steady attack. Each year, metre by metre, the sea takes its due. The mapmakers of the 18th and 19th centuries, when they drew their sandy lines and curling spits, etched these land-sea boundaries many metres north of today's beaches and dunes.

Blakeney Eye is a small sandy island (or 'eye') rising several feet above the marsh on the landward side of a bend in the Cley Channel. At its northernmost tip are the remains of a chapel, referred to as Blakeney Chapel on present day maps. It's late summer and I'm back in Blakeney. I have decided to walk along the raised banks of sea defences to take a look at the ruins. The 'island' and the remains of its chapel are surrounded by channels and creeks. A stiff, chill wind is blowing from the north. It whips urgent, white crested waves that petulantly rattle up the shingle. The ruins are 190 metres from the edge of the sea at low tide. But go back a couple of hundred years and low tide is mapped at twice the distance, 400 metres away to the north of the ruined chapel. This is a coastline in retreat, albeit, courtesy of the Environment Agency, a 'managed retreat'. Two hundred years hence, there will be no chapel, and only those who have a fondness for old maps will ponder the sea's restless appetite and nature's indifference to our efforts.

Each year the marshes and creeks narrow as they are pushed a little nearer to North Norfolk's line of east-west running hills and low glacial ridges. Nevertheless, in the sea's constant war of attrition, the once thriving ports have proved resilient and adaptive. They are today's pretty villages and holiday destinations. They are the location of choice for many small businesses and creative enterprises. I take a lingering look at the overgrown ruins of the chapel before making my way back to Blakeney for lunch. The sharp wind is now behind me. The grasses rustle and sway. A few determined reed warblers dart and dash low across the marshes. The sky darkens. I eat my fish pie with the sound of heavy rain rattling against the restaurant windows. Blakeney Point, the ruined chapel and distant sea become lost amongst the low, rushing, stormy grey clouds.

Plate 1: Albert Einstein – painting on promenade café wall, Sheringham

Plate 2: Albert Einstein, with Commander Locker-Lampson, Miss Billing and the local game-keeper, by his hut on Roughton Heath.
© London Science Museum's Science and Society Picture Library

Plate 3: Hunstanton: Chalk and Carstone cliffs

Plate 4: Hunstanton cliffs: close up of Cretaceous Carstones, Red Chalk and White Chalk

Plate 5: Sir Thomas Browne: statue, Hay Hill, Norwich

Plate 6: Blakeney Point, North Norfolk
© Mike Page Photography, Mike-Page.co.uk

Plate 7: Holkham Beach, North Norfolk

Plate 8: ALBATROS, sailing clipper, quayside, Wells-next-the Sea

Plate 9: Nelson: statue, precincts of Norwich Cathedral

Plate 10: North Elmham, remains of the Norman Chapel, later converted into a small, moated castle built on the site of a timber-structured Anglo-Saxon Cathedral

Plate 11: Remains of Roman market town, Caistor St Edmund, showing the layout of the original street pattern
© Mike Page Photography, Mike-Page.co.uk

Plate 12: Round towered church, St Andrew, Colney

Plate 13: Amelia Opie, figurine statue, Opie Street, Norwich

Plate 14: Robert Kett,
bronze roundel, Norwich
City Hall, main doors

Plate 15: Kett's Oak, B1172, near Wymondham, Norfolk

Plate 16: Thomas Paine, statue, King Street, Thetford

Plate 17: Hickling Broad (top) leading in to Heigham Sound (below). © Mike Page Photography, Mike-Page.co.uk

Plate 18: Looking north along the B1113 between Redgrave and South Lopham, the watershed between the source of the River Waveney to the east (right) and the Little Ouse River to the west (left)

Plate 19: Margaret Fountaine. © Norfolk Museums Service

Plate 20: Julian of Norwich, statue,
West Door, Norwich Cathedral

Plate 21: Igneous erratics which hitched a 400-mile ride aboard the Anglian Ice Sheet, half a million years ago, now on Cromer beach

Plate 22: 'flint squared' wall

and

'flint knapped random' wall

DEW YEW LOOK UP!

We can't show yew a mount'n,
An, bor, we're short o'hills,
An' yew oon't taake long a'countin'
Ar caastles an' ar mills.
But don't yew set there sighin' –
Jus' caast yar oyes up high
Where clouds an' baads are flyin',
An' see ar Norfick Sky!

(John Kett, Norfolk dialect poet)

Plate 23: Norfolk sky

Chapter 8
Sailors and Sinners

Travelling west from Cley, Blakeney and Wells, we see the same story of silting and retreat repeated at Burnham Overy, Brancaster Staithe and Thornham. Not that the word retreat was ever part of the vocabulary of Horatio Nelson, but looking out across Burnham Overy Staithe today, instead of the commercial ships of the mid-18th century, all he would see are sailing dinghies and the (virtual) home of the Overy Staithe Sailing Club whose web page gives visiting sailors approaching the creek the following welcome and encouraging advice:

> There is no formal buoyage. There are no lights. Visitors should be wary of stone-built groynes sticking out into the creek…Mobile phone coverage is patchy… Facilities in Overy Staithe are limited to the chandlery and a pub…This may look a little bit off-putting, and in a way, it's meant to be. On the other hand, it's a beautiful spot, accessible (with care) in daylight, on a reasonably big tide, and when there isn't too much sea running from the north.

All the villages in this area, including Burnham Market, take their name from the little River Burn. It flows north down the glacial tills and boulder clays before disappearing into the creeks and channels of Burnham Overy Staithe, a staithe being a waterside landing stage.

In medieval times, the main port was in fact at Burnham Overy Town where the River Burn could still be navigated by sea-going ships and barges. But as the seas rose and the silting took place, the main port migrated half a mile down river, north to Overy Staithe where Nelson might have seen small cargo boats being loaded and unloaded and fisherman returning with their catch.

Nelson was born in 1758 in the Rectory situated half a mile to the south of Burnham Thorpe, a hamlet straddling the River Burn a couple of miles inland. Nelson's father, Edmund, was the vicar for the Burnhams. He was married to Catherine Suckling. Catherine's own mother, Ann, was the daughter of Sir Charles Turner, a wealthy merchant from King's Lynn and Mary Walpole of Houghton Hall, Norfolk. The Hall was built in the 1720s by Sir Robert Walpole, who served as Prime Minister between 1721 and 1742; twenty one years and still a record. This made Catherine the grandniece of Sir Robert Walpole. So, although Horatio's father, Edmund, came from a modest but gentrified background of farmers and clergymen, his mother's family was altogether grander, with good connections both politically and financially

It was these connections that helped Edmund Nelson become Vicar of Burnham Thorpe. The Walpoles owned considerable land and properties in the Burnham area. So it was that when Thomas Smithson, the rector of Burnham Thorpe, died in 1755, the Walpole influence came into play. Horace (Horatio) Walpole, Sir Robert's eldest son and heir, ensured that the rectories and livings that went with the Burnham parishes were presented to Edmund.

Horatio Nelson was the sixth of Edmund and Catherine Nelson's eleven children. And it was after the family's benefactor, Lord Horatio Walpole, that Horatio was named. The boy was always called Horace by his family; indeed, even as an adult, he would often sign himself Horace.

When Horace was only nine years old, his mother, Catherine, died. This was a severe blow for the eight children still alive. Their father was grief-stricken and fretted about how he was going to look after his brood. It was eventually decided that Horace and William, a year older than his brother, should be schooled. It was sometime during 1768 that they took their places at the King Edward VI Grammar School in Norwich sited by the Cathedral. They boarded with their paternal aunt, Thomasine, who lived in the city. She was married to John Goulty, a maker of fine leather shoes. They had a five year old son, so there was room in the house for the two nephews. A year later the boys transferred to the Sir William Paston Grammar School in the small market town of North Walsham. The brothers returned home for holidays. William was a bright boy and in 1774 went up to the University of Cambridge destined to follow in the footsteps of his clergyman father.

Horace was the second of the Nelson children to leave home. It was the Christmas holidays of late 1770. Horace was reading the local *Norfolk Chronicle* when he saw a report about the brewing conflict between Spain and Britain over possession of the Falkland Islands far away in the South Atlantic. The Admiralty was commissioning new ships and was anxious to tempt some of its pensioned captains out of retirement. Horace's maternal Uncle, Captain Maurice Suckling, had not been at sea for a number of years. He was a friend of, and support to the Nelson family.

Maurice didn't hesitate at the prospect of returning to sea. In November 1771, he was appointed to the new, sixty-four gun battleship, the *Raisonable*. She was being fitted out at Chatham and it would be several months before she would be ready for action. Excited by events, Horace asked his brother William to write to their father, who was in Bristol at the time, to ask if he would explore with Uncle Maurice the idea of Horace joining the ship under his command.

Although it was always envisaged that one of the Nelson boys would be supported by Uncle Maurice and take up a career at sea, Horace, who had been something of a sickly child, was not seen as the obvious choice. But the boy seemed to have an appetite for adventure and had been inspired by some of his uncle's stories of life aboard ship. So it was agreed that when the warship was ready and the twelve year old Horace had completed another term at Paston Grammar School, he would leave home and join the navy.

After a brief stay in London, Horace went down river to join his Uncle as a midshipman on board the *Raisonable*. Given his background and connections, the boy was seen as an officer-in-training. The ship was still docked and being made ready for sea. During these few preparatory weeks, Horace underwent an intense course of seamanship to get the hang of how life was to be lived aboard a fighting ship with its complement of 500 men.

While all these preparations were taking place, the Spanish and British had managed to sort out some of their Falkland Island differences. As a result, the *Raisonable* was decommissioned and for the time being wouldn't be sailing anywhere. Captain Maurice Suckling was transferred to a larger ship, the *Triumph*. She was seven years old and was armed with 74 guns. Horace was discharged from the *Raisonable* and a day later, on 22 May 1771, he joined his uncle aboard the *Triumph*.

The *Triumph*'s duties, though important, were not likely to give the young Horatio, as we might now call him, much ocean-going experience. She was operating as a guardship sailing mainly in the Thames Estuary and Medway. To help Horatio get a proper sea life, Uncle Maurice intervened once more. The uncle learned that an old friend was soon to sail a merchant ship, the *Mary Ann*, off to the Caribbean. Captain John Rathbone agreed to take Horatio on board and on 25 July 1771, Horatio Nelson, still only twelve years old, set sail for the West Indies.

From that moment, Nelson's experiences at sea became increasingly exotic and varied. On his return from the West Indies, Uncle Maurice found his nephew a place on board a survey ship bound for the Arctic. This wasn't a great success. The ship became temporarily stuck in the ice. From the Arctic, he then sailed to the East with the frigate HMS *Seahorse* where he experienced being under enemy fire for the first time. There followed a rapid succession of expeditions, encounters and new ships. Nelson's talents were recognised and he began to enjoy regular promotions.

It was while in the West Indies during the spring of 1787 that he met and married the young widow Fanny Nesbit. They returned to England. There was a lull in the nation's naval wartime activities. In the summer of 1788, Captain Nelson decided it was time to introduce his wife to the family back home in Norfolk, including his aging, ailing and increasingly frail father.

Horatio and Fanny spent much of the next five years in Burnham Thorpe rectory. Nelson was restless and anxious to get back to sea, but he kept drawing blanks as he sought new commissions. After several setbacks he reluctantly resigned himself to a life in North Norfolk, doing a bit of gardening and having a half-hearted attempt at farming. More positively, the return home allowed Nelson to renew and deepen the relationship with his elderly father.

But then once again, war loomed, this time with France. In 1793, Nelson was back at sea in command of *HMS Agamemnon* on its way to join the fleet in the Mediterranean. Most commentators agree that Nelson was a man driven by ambition and a need to succeed, be recognised and admired. It was this overdue return to sea and the prospect of naval battles that marked the true beginnings of the Horatio Nelson that we know and celebrate today.

Over the next few years Nelson's naval successes in the Mediterranean became legendary. Back home he was rapidly becoming something of a national hero. His daring tactics, the loss of his right eye while trying to help the army capture the island of Corsica at the siege of Calvi in 1794, his swaggering attitude to both friend and foe, only increased his popularity. He was knighted and then promoted to the rank of Rear Admiral. He was not yet forty.

Further sea battles saw him severely wounded in his right arm which had to be amputated. After a brief recuperation he was once again back in the Mediterranean, tracking down and attacking the French Fleet at the Battle of the Nile in August 1798. The victory he achieved resulted in his elevation to Baron. He was now Lord Horatio Nelson.

It was while he was in the friendly port of Naples having his ships repaired after the defeat of the French fleet that Nelson visited the British Ambassador, Sir William Hamilton, and his much younger wife, Lady Emma Hamilton. Even before she met Nelson, Emma had led an interesting, if not to say spirited life.

She was born in Cheshire in 1765. As a 12 year old girl she was working as a maid for Dr Thomas, a Chester-based surgeon. After a move to London, Emma found jobs working as a maid for various Drury Lane actresses. This life also gave her opportunities to model and dance.

Still only a young woman, she became the mistress first of Sir Harry Featherstonehaugh and then Charles Greville. It was Greville who asked his friend George Romney, the fashionable portrait painter, to provide him with a picture of Emma. Romney became fascinated and beguiled by the young woman and for a long time she became his muse. The many paintings of Emma made throughout the 1780s and 90s meant that she became well-known in society circles. She was quickly recognised as a woman of beauty, wit and intelligence.

However, Greville's need for a rich wife led him to abandon Emma. She agreed to visit Naples as the guest of Greville's uncle, the widower Sir William Hamilton, well-known for his hospitality and taste. Unbeknown to Emma, Greville and Sir William had in mind that Emma should become the widower's hostess whenever he held parties at his Neapolitan house, and maybe even become his mistress. Initially, Emma was furious when she learned of their plan, but true to her enterprising nature, she soon became a great success as a hostess, singer, and performer of various classical poses or 'attitudes' as they were known. She was all the rage.

Several years later, in 1791, aged twenty six, she married Sir William Hamilton and so became Lady Emma Hamilton. He was aged sixty, thirty three years her senior. Nelson had actually met Emma briefly in 1793 during a short visit to see Sir William. Five years later, in 1798, Nelson was again back in Naples, docking his battled-bruised, but victorious ship. He accepted an invitation to stay with Sir William and his wife at their home, the Palazzo Sessa. After many years of fighting at sea, Nelson's health was not good and he was in need of care, if not love and attention. Emma took to her nursing duties with enthusiasm and it was not long before she and Nelson became lovers.

Ambassador Hamilton and Nelson appeared to like each other. The aging Sir William apparently tolerated the affair between the famous admiral and his wife. However, as soon as he felt strong enough, Nelson was back on board and back at sea.

The Hamiltons returned to London in 1800. In January 1801, Emma gave birth to Horatia, Nelson's daughter. That same year, Nelson set sail from Great Yarmouth with his fleet towards Denmark and the port of Copenhagen. The Danish fleet and shore-based guns were in waiting.

At first things did not go well and the Fleet Commander signalled 'retreat'. As was often the case, Nelson ignored the signal. His excuse, made to his flag Captain, Thomas Foley, was 'You know, Foley, I have only one eye. I have a right to be blind sometimes.' And with that, he raised his telescope to his blind eye and famously said 'I really do not see the signal.' The battle was ferocious and ended in a truce. As a further reward for his naval successes, on 19 May 1801, Horatio was created Viscount Nelson of the Nile and of Burnham Thorpe in the County of Norfolk.

Sir William Hamilton died in 1803. The only thing preventing Nelson and Emma marrying was the social opprobrium likely to follow any attempt by Nelson to divorce his dutiful wife, Fanny. Meanwhile, Emma was pregnant once more, but their second daughter, only a few weeks old, died in 1804. With Nelson at sea, Emma was lonely, distressed and growing increasingly dissolute. She was over-eating, over-spending, and gambling recklessly.

And finally for Nelson, the Battle of Trafalgar. On 20 October 1805, Napoleon's navy was spotted leaving Cadiz harbour. The next day, Nelson, aboard *HMS Victory*, ordered his ships to head towards the enemy and engage them in battle. The British fleet was steeled by the last signal he ever sent: 'England expects every man will do his duty.' The French and British forces met off Cape Trafalgar down in the far south western corner of Spain's Atlantic coast.

The battle was fierce. The ships fought at close quarters. Casualties were high on both sides. It was in the middle of all this violence that Nelson was shot by a sniper firing from the French ship *Redoutable*. The wound was fatal. As his life ebbed away, Nelson was attended by the captain of the *Victory*, Thomas Hardy along with the ship's chaplain, surgeon, purser and steward.

Nelson was given a state funeral. On a winter's day, 9 January 1806, the procession marched slowly from the Admiralty to St Paul's Cathedral. The crowds were huge. Politicians and royalty, admirals and sea captains, and thousands of soldiers and sailors escorted the hero to his final resting place. The only person missing was Emma Hamilton, forbidden to attend by the state's authorities.

Nelson's coffin was made from the timbers of the *L'Orient*, one of the defeated French ships at the Battle of the Nile. Today the coffin sits inside a deep, black marble sarcophagus, originally made for Cardinal Wolsey, Lord Chancellor during the reign of Henry VIII. Wolsey had fallen from favour and the unused sarcophagus was stored at Windsor for nearly 300 years until a fitting subject could be found. Nelson's viscount coronet now sits on top of the magnificent tomb which can be seen in the crypt of St Paul's. It stands only a few yards along from Arthur Wellesley, the Duke of Wellington's equally imposing tomb carved from Cornish granite. And just round the corner from the two of them, occupying a more modest resting place, is the tomb of the architectural genius of St Paul's itself, Sir Christopher Wren. Nelson and Wellington can also be found in the precincts of Norwich Cathedral. (See *Plate 9*) They face in opposite directions. Nelson's statue gazes north, while less than a hundred yards across the lawn Wellington's eyes are cast forever south.

Although permanent neighbours in death, Nelson and Wellington only met once in life. The brief encounter took place on 12 September 1805 at the Colonial Office in Downing Street in the outer office of the State Secretary for War, Lord Castlereagh. The next day, Nelson left to join *HMS Victory* and sailed south to Cape Trafalgar. Seven weeks later he was dead.

In 2005, two hundred years after the Rear-Admiral's death, his home county made the decision to celebrate its most famous son by giving its road signs a makeover. As you enter the county by any of its major routes, the border signs now read 'NORFOLK: Nelson's County'. If Shakespeare was good enough for Warwickshire, then Nelson would certainly do for Norfolk.

After her lover's death, Emma Hamilton's final years became increasingly difficult. She was snubbed by society. She ran into debt and moved to France to escape her creditors. There she lived a life of poverty. She died in 1815 of amoebic dysentery. Horatia, the couple's only surviving daughter, clearly playing safe and seeking a life of quiet respectability, returned to England and married the Reverend Philip Ward. They had ten children, the firstborn of which they named Horatio Nelson.

History has treated Emma Hamilton more kindly than the society of her day. Her rise from poverty, her intelligence, social skill, passion and resilience make modern audiences far more sympathetic to her character and career than the hypocritical reaction shown by Georgian England. Kate Williams, her biographer, sees her as 'a true heroine'. Today, a painting of her hangs next to one of Nelson in the National Portrait Gallery, within 'kissing distance' as Simon Sharma sweetly puts.

Film makers, too, have had a rare old time telling the story of Emma's rise and fall, and her passionate affair with Nelson. The 1968 film, *Emma Hamilton*, was made by the French director Christian-Jaque starring Michèle Mercier as Emma, the Essex raised Richard Johnson as Nelson, and the Norfolk born John Mills as the cuckholded Sir William Hamilton. Sir John Mills appeared in over a hundred films. He was born in the little village of North Elmham, a few miles west of Norwich. Nelson's youngest brother, Suckling, had lived in the hamlet with his new bride and may well have received a visit from Horatio and his wife in 1788 when they were doing the rounds of the Norfolk relations. However, Suckling's marriage and attempts at running a grocery business in North Elmham both failed and he soon drifted back to Burnham Thorpe.

John Mills' mother gave birth to her son in 1908 in the staff quarters at the Watts Naval School where his father was a mathematics teacher. The building was originally the Norfolk County School, a public school founded in 1873 by Prebendary Joseph Brereton, rector of Little Massingham, Norfolk. The original school's aim was to cater for the educational needs of the sons of farmers and artisans. But the school was not a success and closed in 1895.

The school was then sold to Edward Watts whose son, Fenwick, refurbished it and gifted it to Dr Barnardo's Homes. In 1903, the magnificent brick and flint buildings and extensive grounds became both home and school for around 300 boys whose parents could not, should not or would not look after them because of death, poverty, illness, neglect or abuse. Although some fifteen miles from the sea, the school aimed to train the boys to become sailors and seamen for the merchant and royal navies – hence its new name, the Watts Naval Training School.

The headteachers were from a naval background and were addressed as Captain or Commander. Not surprisingly, the school ran with a strong nautical flavour. A tall ship's mast acted as the school's flagpole. The main hall was known as The Quarter Deck. As well as conventional lessons there were morning inspections, prayers, drills, swimming, splicing, knotting, and 'the general handling of ropes'. Dr Barnado's Homes themselves believed four or five years at the school would fit the boys for a career at sea and, as the charity's house magazine of the day went on to say, 'to earn their own living and do their duty as Nelson did.'

The School closed in 1953. Most of the buildings were demolished. The site is now mainly one of woods and grassy fields. However, the Captain's house remains, and the chapel survives as a private home, alongside a number of other converted family houses. The old school grounds slope west down to the River Wensum – wend-sum, the winding, wending river. On the opposite bank, also just north of North Elmham's main cluster of houses, lie other ruins, much older. These are the remains of a Bishop's Palace and the site of an Anglo-Saxon Cathedral.

Christianity was introduced into the British Isles towards the end of the Roman occupation in the 3rd and 4th centuries. However, throughout much of Anglo-Saxon England, Christianity remained a minority faith. Pagan beliefs were still enthusiastically embraced by most of the population, boosted, of course, by invasions from the east by the Angles, Saxons and Jutes many of whom settled in East Anglia.

It was not until Christianity was linked to kingship in the 6th century that the faith became more widespread. The first bishop of the East Angles was Felix, a priest from Burgundy. He was praised by the Venerable Bede for rescuing the Anglo-Saxon pagans from the many paths of 'unrighteousness'. The details of Felix's ministry are hazy, but it is thought that he arrived in the area around 630 AD and established his See somewhere in Suffolk, possibly based at the coastal port of Dunwich or maybe Walton near Felixstowe. Coastal erosion has washed away both these sites and no traces of his headquarters remain though the port of Felixstowe is a modern-day reminder of the saint's presence and importance.

By the 8th century, England was probably just about more Christian than pagan. However, further 9th century invasions from the east, this time by Danish and Norwegian Vikings, saw a return of pagan beliefs across many parts of the country. In the end it took King Alfred's successful dealings with the invaders to confirm Christianity as the established faith.

Norfolk was a prosperous region in Late Saxon times. The county was well populated and building a church in your 'parish' was a symbol of piety, status and success. By the 10th century, local landowners were enthusiastically building places of worship all over the county. However, the English Saxons had no tradition of building in stone. Most of their churches were timber framed, built of wood, wattle-and-daub and clay lump. Few remains of these places of worship survive today.

The Episcopal centre of these late Saxon times was the little Norfolk village of North Elmham. Indeed, for several hundred years up until 1071 North Elmham was where the Bishops, their See and Episcopal throne were based. Technically speaking, therefore, the North Elmham church, though small and made mainly of wood, was nevertheless regarded as the county's cathedral.

In 1071, after the Norman conquest of 1066, the first Norfolk-based bishop to be appointed by the Normans, Bishop Herfast, moved his headquarters from North Elmham to Thetford. At the time, Thetford was both prosperous and well populated.

But in 1090, the new Diocesan Bishop of Thetford, William de Beaufeu, died. Bishoprics were prized positions, coming with great lands and wealth. Any bishop-elect was expected to pay a good price to the King, William II, Rufus, for the vacancy of a vacant See.

Herbert de Losinga was an ambitious Normandy born priest. He was willing to pay the going price for the Norfolk See even though he knew that according to church beliefs and law, the purchase of any ecclesiastical or spiritual office was corrupt and sinful, the sin being that of simony. In the clash between Herbert's faith and his ambition, ambition won. He paid a thousands marks to the King and was consecrated Bishop of Thetford in 1091.

However, Thetford's days as a cathedral city were short-lived. Although a skilful, scholarly man, de Losinga's mind did not rest easy with the manner of his rise and promotion. At the time, relations between the Pope, the English King and his Norman born bishops were not good. Herbert de Losinga knew that Urban II was a reforming Pope, and sensibly enough Herbert, now Bishop of Thetford, had written tracts that were proving helpful to Pope Urban in his wish to bring about a number of changes in church practices.

On a visit to Rome, Herbert de Losinga, seeking absolution from his sin of simony, humbly resigned his post as Bishop. He was then absolved of all his sins by the Pope, and immediately re-instated as Bishop of Thetford. What other penances he promised in order to amend his sins is not known, but speculations down the centuries have suggested that one of Herbert's commitments was to build a bigger and better cathedral in his diocese.

The Bishop kept his promise and so began the construction of a new cathedral, made of stone, using the latest and best Norman masonry skills. A few years earlier, the Archbishop of Canterbury, Lanfranc, had ordered that Sees should be moved to the busiest centres of economic activity in each diocese. Herbert de Losinga therefore decreed that the cathedral should be built in Norwich which was emerging as a booming centre with a fast growing population, thought to number around six thousand souls. The transfer of his headquarters in 1094 also meant that the Bishop of Thetford now became the Bishop of Norwich. The first stone of the new cathedral was laid in 1096.

However, Bishop de Losinga still had the little village of North Elmham in mind. On the site of the old wooden Saxon cathedral he built a stone chapel as well as a new parish church.

A couple of centuries later, the site and the chapel underwent one further identity change. One of the leading figures in the brutal suppression of the 1381 Norfolk-branch of the Peasants Revolt was another Bishop of Norwich, Henry le Despencer. His actions were viewed with anger and resentment by the general peasantry and he began to worry about his safety. The chapel at North Elmham, originally built by Herbert de Losinga, proved an ideal place to which the Bishop might retreat at times of danger and stress, so he turned it into a fortified manor house. It was enlarged. He built turrets. He dug a moat. In fact most of what we see today around the site of the original wooden cathedral are the ruins of this 'chapel-castle' makeover. (See *Plate 10*)

It's August and I'm having a wander round the ruins. They are not much to look at but they have much to tell. As the sun warms the ragged walls, I'm entertained by the thought that, as so often is the case, good can come from bad. A corrupt bishop, wishing to atone for the sin of simony, builds a beautiful cathedral. Two centuries later, another bishop's violent reprisals and subsequent fears for his own safety scare him into building a grand fortified house whose ruins today are treasured by English Heritage.

There were certainly a great number of churches in 11th century Norfolk. The growing wealth and population of late Saxon times accounted for much of this building boom. Almost every village had its place of worship. Competition between neighbouring parishes in which having a church was seen as a symbol of success and status added further impetus to the building fervour.

Over the next few centuries the county's continued prosperity saw more and more churches being built. Even today, Norfolk has more churches by far than any other county in the country. Of the 800 or more originally built, many of course, have become redundant. Nevertheless, as you wander the pathways, bridleways and lanes, you are constantly struck, not just by the number of churches but in many cases, by their size and beauty.

It was George Borrow who, while scanning Norwich and its cathedral from the higher ground of Mousehold Heath, declared that it was 'a fine old city…gazing from those heights, the eye beholds a scene which cannot fail to awaken.' Rather taken with Borrow's description, Norwich City Council adopted Borrow's sentiment as a strapline for its signage. As you enter the city by any of its major roads today you pass a sign that says:

Welcome to
NORWICH
A FINE CITY

Equally effusive is the Pevsner guide to *The Buildings of England*. 'Norwich,' it declares, 'has everything – a cathedral. A major castle on a mound right in the middle, walls and towers, an admittedly disturbed medieval centre with winding streets and alleys, thirty-five medieval parish churches, and a river with steamships (even if only small ones) and with motor-yachts and sailing boats.' And just in case Noel Coward enthusiasts are still not convinced, the guide adds 'It even has hills.'

The Cathedral of the Holy and Undivided Trinity, to give its full name, lies on a low flood plain by the River Wensum in Norwich twenty five miles downstream from the original diocesan Saxon cathedral built on the banks of the same river at North Elmham. Although plans for a cathedral in the city probably go back to the 1080s, the first stone was laid in 1096. The building was constructed at some speed and was completed by 1145.

Being a cathedral of size and importance, no local materials were thought good enough for the job, at least for outward appearances. And being Norman and already having experience of building large churches, the decision was made to use the pale creamy Caen limestone from Normandy for the cathedral's facing stone. This is a fine-grained rock and therefore easily cut, shaped and carved.

Caen limestone was laid down in the Jurassic period, some 167 million years ago. The oldest exposed rocks in Norfolk are also Jurassic, outcropping in the far west of the county. But they are a poor relation of their fine French cousin, at least for building purposes. The rocks of late Jurassic Norfolk are represented by a thin strip of soft mudstones and most of them lie hidden beneath the Fens and the sandy and clay debris of the last Ice Age. So Caen limestone it had to be.

The stone was quarried in France, shipped north past the coasts of Kent, Essex and Suffolk before turning left at Great Yarmouth. Here the ships would navigate the River Yare to the point where it is joined by the River Wensum on the eastern outskirts of Norwich. A right turn up the Wensum and sailing another mile or so finally brought the limestone to the centre of the city and a few hundred yards from where the cathedral was being built. And to make life even easier, a special canal was then cut from the river to the construction site taking the stone on the last leg of its journey. Even after the cathedral had been built the canal continued to be used to bring fuel up to the priory's kitchens to keep the fires burning and the cathedral monks well fed.

The canal was eventually filled in about 1772, but there is still an inlet on the river bank over which spans a Water Gate. It was built of flint in the 15th century. Next to it, but built a couple of hundred years later in 1647 is the Ferry House constructed of flint and brick. Today the buildings are usually referred to as Pull's Ferry, named after John Pull who operated a ferry across the river for nearly fifty years between 1796 and 1841.

It's only a short walk from the green on which Nelson and Wellington's statues stand along Cathedral Close, down Ferry Lane following the route of the old canal to Pull's Ferry and the River Wensum. Although it's a rather cold, dreary January afternoon, I'm on a short walk along the path that follows the river. As I approach the Water Gate, I take a seat on a damp bench and look across the water. It hasn't rained much recently and the Wensum's flow is sluggish, almost reluctant as if it couldn't be bothered pushing against the tide's final reach. I get up and re-pass the Water Gate and Ferry House. And as walk by, I run my hand along the brittle flint walls. The stone is glass-smooth. Flint resists weathering like no other stone. But it is a hard material with which to build, but build with it they did, those medieval masons with their skills, craft and patience.

Chapter 9
Invaders and Insurgents

If flint wasn't suitable, or indeed good enough for the cathedral, then it was the stone of choice for most of Norfolk's churches. This takes us back to those warm Cretaceous seas in which the remains of chalky, calcareous and silaceous plankton rained steadily down over millions of years onto the sinking sea floor. It was the dissolving and re-precipitation of the silica-rich plankton and sponges that eventually resulted in the formation of the chalk's famous flint layers.

Now flint might not have been the first choice of the medieval church builder, but in Norfolk it has two major virtues. First, flint can be found everywhere – nodules in the fields, layers in the chalk, stones in the rivers, pebbles on the beach. And second, it is durable. Very, very durable. Sandstones and limestones may look good, may be easy to cut and carve, but over time they weather and crumble. Eventually, the stone blocks and carvings have to be replaced ensuring that the ancient skills and craft of the stonemason are kept alive and well.

In contrast, flint hardly weathers at all. Being made of silica, and having very fine, glass-like qualities mean that it is hard, hard as flint. Of course, these qualities also mean that it is a difficult material with which to work. It is tough to cut. It is impossible to carve. But you can knap it. By using one piece of flint to chip away at another, the nodules can be splintered, shaped, and cut to size. And the technique of knapping goes back a long way. (See *Plate 22* for examples of flint wall work)

Dredged up by trawlers, found on beaches, dug up in fields, any number of Stone Age flint arrows, axe heads and ancient cutting tools have been found by fishermen, archaeologists, farmers, ramblers and beachcombers. When your eyes spot that fractured shape glinting on a beach or piercing a ploughed ridge on the edge of a field, you stop a second as your breath is momentarily taken away. In a gasp, you realise that the flint tool – lost, buried, dropped, abandoned – was last in the hands of some ancient ancestor as he or she was cutting meat, scraping an animal skin, aiming an arrow or guiding a spear.

Although some very rare flint tools might be tens of thousands of years old and may even have been manufactured by our hominid close cousins, the Neanderthals, the vast majority post-date the end of the last Ice Age which ended some 18,000 years ago. And it wasn't until the climate began to warm and the tundra turned lush and temperate that, as we have seen, small bands of hunter-gatherers and proto-farmers began to roam the flood plains and woods of Norfolk and Doggerland. If these early Britons wanted to hunt well, they needed weapons, the sharper, the harder, the better. Flint proved ideal.

Flints are stones and the fashioning of stones into implements and tools takes us back to the Stone Ages – the Mesolithic, from 10,000 to 6,500 years ago, and the Neolithic from 6,500 to 4,300 years ago. The social and cultural changes from hunting and gathering in the Mesolithic, or Middle Stone Age, to the beginnings of farming and the growth of small settlements in the Neolithic, or New Stone Age, is reflected in what was left behind and can be found today. Over time, the weapons and tools became more refined. Pots appeared as people began to settle in one place, farm the land, rear animals, store food, and cook meals.

It is hardly surprising that given their cutting and killing qualities, flints were highly prized. By late Neolithic and early Bronze Age times a brisk and extensive trade in flints had developed. Evidence of this can be seen at Grimes Graves, five miles north west of Thetford and that's where I am today, in Breckland country. I have driven the thirty odd miles from Norwich and parked the car. It's as I approach the Graves that I see the extraordinary landscape of cratered grass, pockmarked and battered, looking for all the world like a vast burial site covering nearly a hundred acres. But it is not a place of the dead. It is the remains of industrial scale flint mining begun some 5,000 years ago.

For hundreds of years, Neolithic miners dug shafts up to thirty feet down into the chalk. They were after the deeper, more precious flint bands where the stone was better for producing sharper and keener tools. Wooden ladders and platforms allowed the men to dig deeper, remove the chalk and mine the flint. Deer antlers were used as picks. Wood was shaped into shovels. And like all miners following a vein, the men of Grimes Graves tunnelled laterally as they chased the flint bands creating galleries that could extend for many metres horizontally into the chalk.

Tons of flint nodules could be won from each digging. On the surface the flint would be knapped into rough shape ready for transport and export, to be traded all over the country. The flint was particularly good for making stone axes and could be exchanged for other goods. It is when the glass-like flint is fractured and knapped that it produces the splinters and edges that are razor sharp.

Grimes Graves is managed by English Heritage. One of the old mine workings has been excavated and restored to something like its original conditions. I pay my entrance fee and look round the small, but excellent exhibition. There is a 30 foot climb down the shaft to the floor below. The chalk is bright white, banded and blocky. The flint layers run in black broken circles round the wall of the mine. A tunnel disappears horizontally beneath the chalk. This is where the ancient flint miners crawled, hacked and fought the rock. Their prize was the pristine, black flint. It's almost impossible for me, in my heavy walking shoes, wearing a thick jacket and trousers, to imagine what it must have been like to work the flint all those thousands of years ago. But work it they did, exporting the rock along the major trade routes that were being carved across the country. Today, most of the workings have been back filled with the chalk spoils and it is this that has produced the extraordinary pummelled, grassy landscape of Grimes Graves that we see today.

In 1792, several thousand years later, flint was once again mined near Brandon in the Grimes Graves area. But this time the flints were not for making axes and spears. They were used in the firing of guns. The striking of flint against steel creates a spark and the spark can ignite gunpowder which can fire a weapon. This mechanism led to the guns of the 18th and early 19th centuries being described as flintlocks.

The great quantity and excellent quality of the Brandon flints meant that they became highly valued in times of warfare. They were certainly used by the Duke of Wellington's soldiers. The hardness, durability and reliability of the Brandon flint has been cited as one of the reasons why Wellington was able to defeat Napoleon at the Battle of Waterloo in 1815.

It was not until the Romans arrived that the building potential of flint was realised. And the thing that made this possible was mortar. The Romans had invented mortar and had been using it for hundreds of years to cement the bricks and stones of their villas, temples, forums, aqueducts and amphitheatres.

Although Julius Caesar had made a flying visit to the country in 55 BC, the Romans didn't seriously set about conquering Britain until 43 AD when the Emperor Claudius sent his armies north. The local Norfolk Iron Age Celtic tribe was the Iceni. Their king, Prasutagus, struck deals with the invaders allowing him to carry on reigning over his people as a client monarch with only a light touch from Rome. The arrangement allowed King Prasutagus to accumulate a good deal of wealth including loans from several Roman financiers.

The Iceni occupied all of modern-day Norfolk, east Cambridgeshire and the northern fringes of Suffolk. Being an

Iron Age tribe, they were skilled craftsmen, able to fashion iron into tools for farming and weapons for fighting, and gold for coins and jewellery. They built in wood and made pots out of clay. But it was the Romans who began to build houses, walls and roads using the local stone which in the case of Norfolk was predominantly the ubiquitous flint.

In AD 60 relations between the Romans and the Iceni took a distinct turn for the worse after the death of King Prasutagus. He had no male heir and left his private wealth to be shared between his two daughters and the new emperor, Nero. But unfortunately, the Romans were not big on human rights and gender equality. They blatantly ignored the King's will.

It was Rome's custom to permit only male heirs to inherit the titles and powers of their fathers. Furthermore, upon the death of a client sovereign, it was Roman practice to incorporate the client state into the Empire. There would be no new king, and certainly no new queen. And there would be no sharing of assets. Rome intended to take all of King Prasutagus's wealth, plunder his lands, and recover its loans. All powers were to be transferred to Rome.

And just in case the Iceni were not getting the message about who was now in charge, the Roman army tracked down King Prasutagus's wife, Queen Boudica (or Boadicea, as the Victorians called her). She was flogged and her two daughters raped.

Such brutality and humiliation outraged the Iceni and their widowed queen. Fired up with anger and indignation, the Iceni under the leadership of Queen Boudica, organised themselves and revolted. Tens of thousands of tribesmen raged south. They succeeded in sacking the Roman town of Colchester (Camulodonum) in Essex. They rode on and burnt and destroyed London (Londinium) and St Albans (Verulamium) killing citizens and soldiers without mercy.

The Roman Governor of England at the time was Gaius Suetonius Paulus. He'd been over in Anglesey dealing with the western tribes when Boudica made her first move. After hurrying back and deciding that he didn't have the numbers to defend London, he re-grouped his forces in the West Midlands.

The Iceni, possibly less tactically savvy than the Romans, decided to go after their Latin enemy and marched west to meet them. Although superior in numbers, the Iceni lacked the equipment and manoeuvrability of the Roman forces. Queen Boudica, her army, and allies were finally defeated at the Battle of Watling Street in the Midlands. Their territory, including Norfolk, was reconquered.

Boudica, Queen of the Iceni, is celebrated in history as a warrior queen, a British patriot, who fought the Roman Empire. There is a magnificent bronze statue of her by Thomas Thorneycroft first installed in 1902. It rests on a plinth on Victoria Embankment at the western end of Westminster Bridge, opposite the Houses of Parliament, beneath Big Ben. Boudica is riding a scythed chariot pulled by two rearing horses. She holds a spear in her hand and is flanked by her two daughters.

It is perhaps ironic that she is often championed by those who see themselves descended from true English Anglo-Saxon stock. She fought to rid these islands of the Roman occupying forces. If she and her Norfolk tribesmen had lived a few centuries later, no doubt they would have fought equally vigorously to repel the Angles and Saxons who would soon be invading the county from the east across the North Sea.

After Boudica's tribal rebellions, the Romans decided to tighten control over this revolting region, militarily and administratively. They built a local capital just south of Norwich – Venta Icenorum ('the market town of the Iceni') – though quite why here is not certain. It was built on fields by the River Tas just before it flows into the River Yare. The streets were planned on a rectangular grid system. In its heyday during the 2nd and 3rd centuries AD, the town had a population of several thousand.

On current maps you can find Venta Icenorum marked just to the south west of Caistor St Edmund. Little remains of the place save for some hefty flint, chalk and tile defensive walls. But should you find yourself flying high above the old town at the end of a long, hot, dry summer, you will see the old grid pattern outlined below where the parched grass etches out the streets in wonderfully evocative detail. (See *Plate 11*)

And if you don't fly that much over these parts, then any train journey to London from Norwich will reward you with a splendid view of the square of raised ground that marks the remains of the old town walls. Three and a half miles into your southbound journey, facing the engine, look left out of the window. As you gaze across the River Tas, there you will see a beautifully clear square of raised grassy earth, often dotted with grazing sheep. Each side of the square is just under 500 yards long. The raised square defines the town's boundary. At odd points around the perimeter, weathering and archaeological excavations reveal fragments of the original wall itself.

It's wonderful to think that almost two millennia ago you would be looking out, not from a train window, but from the slopes of a river bank across a busy market town, with a temple, forum and baths. And to clinch the picture, just outside the town walls, you would see an amphitheatre whose remains have recently been unearthed. It is possible to walk along the top of the old raised ground. You get a strong sense of times very different and long ago.

Roman rule in Norfolk hung around for a few centuries, but as the Empire began to fall, these northern outposts increasingly found themselves under Barbarian threat. There were attempts by the Romans to defend Norfolk against invasions from these North German tribes. Coastal forts were built at Caister-by-Sea on the east coast and Brancaster (Branodunum) on the north to ward off and defend the country, but ultimately to no avail.

By the early 5th century, it was all over for the Romans in Britain. The invasions saw influxes of people from North

Germany and Denmark, including the Angles from Schleswig-Holstein, the Saxons from the Elbe and Wesser valleys, and the Jutes from Denmark.

In time, the land settled by these invading tribes became known as Engla Lond – the land of the Angles – England. And to distinguish these freshly settled immigrants from the old Saxons of North Germany they had left behind, the newcomers became known as the Anglo-Saxons. And it is their language, Old English, that forms the basis of our modern English.

At first, the invaders arrived piecemeal. There were no attempts to develop clearly defined territories led by tribal chiefs. However, by the end of the 6th century, as competition and conflict set in and alliances forged, a kingdom gradually emerged. This was the land of the East Angles and it fell under the overlordship of the Wuffingas and their dynasty. In the north of the kingdom lived the North Folk (Norfolk, of course) and in the south, the South Folk (Suffolk).

By the 8th century, regional conflicts, battles and land grabs eventually saw the Kings of Mercia in the Midlands assume sovereignty over East Anglia. Norfolk remained primarily an area of farming and small communities. Many modern place names suggest their Anglo-Saxon origins. Any town or village whose name ends in '-ton' or '-tun' or '-ham' or '-thorp' or '-thwaite', or which have '-inga' in their composition hint at Saxon origins. Mulbarton, Reepham, Sheringham, Hunstanton, Walsingham, Fakenham, East Dereham, Wymondham, Ashwellthorpe, North Walsham, and Roughton to name just a few.

The suffix *wic* suggests a place where things were made or sold. Many tended to be slightly larger than the villages (*hams*) or small farms and settlements (*tons*). Keswick, for example, was a place that made cheese. Hardwick was where you might find sheep. And the prosperous town in the north of the region, of course, was named *nor-wic*, Norwich.

No doubt with Boudica doing yet another turn in her grave, 9th century Norfolk suffered further invasions, this time from Danish Vikings. Raids and battles began in the 860s. By the end of the 9th century, the Vikings had established a number of settlements, especially in the east of the county. Place names ending in –*by* give us a clue about where the Vikings chose to calm down, settle, farm, do business, integrate, and finally assimilate. Scratby, Hemsby and Filby are reminders of where these once-feared invaders laid down their weapons and became farmers and traders but not before some bloody conflicts had been waged.

In 869, a battle took place at Thetford between the East Anglian Saxon king, Edmund, and the Vikings. Edmund was defeated, captured and put to a brutal death. East Anglia fell under Viking rule or 'Dane Law'. Further battles with the rest of Saxon England under the leadership of King Alfred eventually lead to a truce. For a while, a period of peace allowed the Vikings to settle amongst the native Saxon population with many of them also converting to Christianity.

By now there was a growing popular belief that the defeated Edmund had not only been a king but also a saint. A mere 20 years after Edmund's violent death, his victors were living peaceably amongst the Anglo-Saxons, practising Christian worship, and recognising Edmund as a martyr. However, for the next couple of centuries, times of peace were often short-lived. Further raids and take-overs by Danish kings and their armies continued to trouble the region.

For example, in 1013, East Anglia surrendered to King Sweyn (Forkbeard) of Denmark, son of King Harald Bluetooth. The English King, Ethelred, fled abroad leaving Sweyn Forkbeard as the first Danish King of England, albeit for only a few weeks before he died in 1013.

Although Sweyn's son Harald II succeeded him, it was his younger son, Cnut, who earned the support of the men of the Danish fleet in England. They proclaimed Cnut King of

England. Hearing of this, Ethelred was encouraged to return from his exile in Normandy and oust Cnut. This he did in 1014. But two years later, Cnut was back. In 1016, he finally managed to become King Cnut, not only of England but eventually also of Denmark, Norway, and parts of Sweden.

In most accounts, Cnut, or Canute as he is sometimes known, is seen as a successful king. He was canny and realistic as evidenced by the story, probably apocryphal, of his attempt to turn back the tide. Of course his command that the waves rise no further failed. He got wet, and so revealed to those about him that the power of kings is limited. 'Let all men know how empty and worthless is the power of kings, for there is none worthy of the name, but He whom heaven, earth, and sea obey by eternal laws' said Cnut, or so records Henry of Huntington a century later. Cnut died, not by drowning but of natural causes in 1035, aged probably in his mid-forties.

Cnut's own sons, first Harold Harefoot, then Harthacnut carried on the family tradition of ruling England for another 26 years, before Edward the Confessor, of the Anglo-Saxon House of Wessex was eventually returned to the throne in 1042. By 1066 Edward, too, was dead, killed by a series of strokes.

Edward's brother-in-law, Harold Godwinson, the Earl of Wessex, was contentiously named as his successor. He was the last Anglo-Saxon King of England, King Harold II. Fearing rival claims for the throne from both the King of Norway and William Duke of Normandy, Harold speedily arranged for his coronation to take place at Westminster Abbey on 6 January, 1066, the day after Edward the Confessor's death. Harold's fears were well founded.

A few months later, King Harald Hardrada of Norway with the support of Harold's disaffected brother Tostig Godwinson, Earl of Northumberland, invaded England. The newly crowned King Harold II and his army marched north to meet them. On 25 September, The King of Norway and his army were roundly beaten by Harold at the Battle of Stamford Bridge, eight miles east of York.

Then the second threat materialised. William, Duke of Normandy sailed across the Channel and landed his army on the Sussex coast. Harold, with a depleted, tired and battle-weary army, rushed south. This time his military efforts were not successful. On 14 October 1066, at the Battle of Hastings, King Harold II died, an arrow through his eye, the last of the Saxon kings. After dealing with a weak rebellion by Edgar Aetheling, The Duke of Normandy, had himself crowned King William I of England at Westminster Abbey on 25 December 1066, the first of the Norman kings.

Over the next couple of years, King William I, The Conqueror, successfully dealt with various attempts by the defeated Danish kings and princes to regain power. By 1070, he was ready to consolidate his conquest and assert control, first in wood and then in stone. Norman castles and cathedrals began to appear across the land. Building work on Norwich Castle commenced sometime between 1066 and 1075. But even more politically canny than building defensive castles and cathedrals to God, William also confiscated huge amounts of land from the defeated English nobles and gifted them to his own men who were variously honoured. They became his 'tenants-in-chief'.

The point of this brief history is to get to the time when the idea of Norfolk as a geographical and administrative entity was finally realised. In no time at all, the Normans were tidying up the political, economic and administrative life of the country. Under the Normans, the land occupied by the North folk of East Anglia was formally recognised as the county of Norfolk. Norwich became the main centre for regional trade and commerce. It was also the centre of Norman power, awesomely made manifest by the building of the impressive royal castle and a few years later, the new cathedral. It is also a reminder that

Norfolk, positioned as it is along the exposed North Sea coast facing the Netherlands, Germany, Denmark and Scandinavia is an easy target for would-be attackers.

We have already noted that the county has been invaded by ice sheets, Romans, Angles, Saxons, Vikings, Normans, and the sea itself as global temperatures increase and water levels rise. Although the number of would-be invaders has lessened over the last thousand years, nevertheless the long, vulnerable coastline of East Anglia has remained a temptation to friend and foe alike. In the early 19th century it was feared that ships of the Napoleonic navy might attack the East Anglian shores. Watchtowers were built on hills and high ground. But it was not until the Great War of 1914-18 that enemy fire actually managed to hit Norfolk, as much by accident as design.

The Imperial German Navy, as well as ships, was also responsible for deploying the new metal framed airships known as Zeppelins. These were massive in size, cylindrical in shape and typically several hundred feet long. They were propelled at speeds of up to 50 to 60 mph by several engines slung beneath the frame. To make them buoyant, they were filled with the highly flammable gas, hydrogen. Hydrogen is good for lift, but the merest spark will ignite it as the Zeppelin Hindenberg, the largest airship ever built, found to its cost as it exploded in flames while attempting to land at Lakehurst, New Jersey, on 6 May 1937. Thirty five passengers died in the inferno.

The Kaiser agreed that the airships could be used to drop bombs on the industrial and military zones around the Thames and Humber estuaries. But flying these monsters of the air was a new art. Knowing where you were and how to get where you wanted to go was not yet an exact science, especially if you were flying at night. In short, more often than not the earliest Zeppelins had only the roughest of ideas where they were. It was easy to mistake one set of lights on a coastline for another. This is what happened when the first raids on the British coast were launched.

On 19 January 1915, three Zeppelins took off from Fuhlsbűttel in Germany. Each was loaded with bombs and incendiary devices. But the weather was not good, and one of the airships turned back. The remaining two headed on across the North Sea.

One, commanded by Leutnant Hans Fritz, arrived on the Norfolk coast and headed south towards the Thames estuary. From the air, the lights of Great Yarmouth might look like any other industrial port, and so Fritz dropped his bombs on the hapless town. Some of the bombs failed to explode or landed harmlessly. However, one high explosive hit St Peter's Plain, damaging a number of nearby buildings. It also killed Martha Taylor and the shoemaker Sam Smith. This couple have the dubious distinction of becoming the first two civilians in Britain ever to be killed in an air raid attack. Of the several bombs dropped over Great Yarmouth that night, the last one landed on a large black dog. We don't know its name. The dog therefore has the equally unfortunate distinction of becoming the first pet to be killed in an air raid attack.

The second Zeppelin, commanded by the generously named Count Magnus von Platen-Hallermund, supposedly bound for the Humber Estuary, found itself flying along the North Norfolk coast, equally uncertain about its exact location. Incendiary bombs were dropped on the innocent, well-mannered town of Sheringham causing considerable damage but no deaths or injuries.

The airship continued to rumble west bombing empty fields around Brancaster Staithes and Hunstanton. Then the Zeppelin turned south. Many of its bombs failed to detonate as it flew over the towns and villages of Heacham, Sandringham, Dersingham, and finally King's Lynn where two more deaths occurred, those of young Percy Goate, aged 14 and Alice Gazeley, aged 26. Poor Alice. Only three weeks earlier her husband had been killed on the battlefields of France. There was damage to property but it was the death of the two young people which caused the greatest shock and outrage.

These two, off-course, hushed giants of the sky, having broken into British air space and having dropped their bombs over Norfolk, finally turned east and headed for Germany back across the North Sea.

Count Magnus von Platen-Hallermund, keen to impress the people back home with his daring-do exploits over 'fortress' Norfolk wrote a combat report that said he had successfully warded off barrages of dangerous anti-aircraft fire. In reality though, so surprised and unprepared were the people of Norfolk, that not a single shot was fired at the Zeppelins. But karma, with quiet patience, long memory and wrathful symmetry, proved to be at play. The Count was killed in a British air raid attack on Hamburg on 21 July 1943.

Nowadays other than the sea's unrelenting progress, the only invasions of Norfolk are benign, or relatively benign. Tourists, seal spotters, bird watchers, and second-home owners are the only ones to flood the county. Many of those who buy their weekend cottages and convert barns work and get rich in London. That's where today's wealth is made. However, in medieval England, it was Norfolk that was rich and for several centuries Norwich came only second to London in size and prosperity. And much of this wealth was expressed in rocks and stones, churches and chapels.

Chapter 10
Wool and Wealth

I'm a fair weather cyclist and today the sun is shining, the wind is light and the forecast is good. The plan is to visit just a few local medieval churches. Within twenty minutes of leaving home I'm cycling along the track that takes me up to the tiny, neat, round towered church of All Saints, Keswick. It stands inviting and silhouetted on top of rising ground that slopes down to the River Yare to the north and the fields above Keswick Hall, one time home of the Gurney family, whom we'll be meeting more formally in a few pages time, to the south. But I am in for a surprise. All is not quite as it seems. Much of the original church was demolished around 1597 and only the ruined walls of the chancel and nave remain. Most of what I can see today was built, often using some of the original stones, in the 1890s by the Gurney family and possibly used as mortuary chapel. It is now a place of worship for the Anglican Church. Holy Communion is held once a month. Thus, my first attempt at exploring Norfolk's medieval past is largely thwarted which is not to say that All Saints, on the hill, isn't a delightful gem, albeit Victorian. So I ride on.

It's less than a couple of miles before I park my bike against the yew tree close to the doors of St Peter's church, Cringleford. And another surprise. Well at least for those of us with a geological turn of mind. At first sight the church walls are built of the ubiquitous flint. No surprise there. But every so often, amongst the flints, are small brown blocks of carstone. This is the rock that we met back in Chapter 4, the self-same coarse rusty Cretaceous sandstone that forms the base of the cliffs at Hunstanton and is used to build the 'gingerbread' houses in the east of the county. What on earth is this rough building stone doing so far west, over forty miles away? Why did the masons bother lugging this rock right across the county? Might it be something to do with St Peter's thousand year history? This venerable old church was established in Saxon times, around 950 AD. Indeed, some of the round headed windows are said to be of Saxon origin. Other parts of the church are Norman and the splendid square tower was built in the 14th century. However, after a wander round both the inside and outside of the church, I am non-the-wiser why medieval stonemasons decided to randomly slot the occasional gingerbread stone in among the flints.

After another couple of miles along the road that runs parallel with the River Yare above its western slopes, passed the hospital and Science Park, I stop by the round towered church of St Andrew, Colney. (See *Plate 12*) It, too, has late Saxon origins. The robust, flint and brick-crenellated tower dates back to around 1050 to 1100. The chancel and nave are a little younger and have been built in the Decorated Gothic style of the 13th and early 14th centuries with much restoration taking place in the Victorian era. Again I spot several small brown carstones dotted in amongst the flints but not as many as I saw at St Peter's. And then yet another surprise. One or two of the larger stones, used as 'quoins' to beef up the corners, are neither flint nor carstone but basalt. Basalt? Basalt is solidified volcanic lava. There are no basalt rocks in Norfolk. There is no lava in East Anglia. Probably the nearest outcrops are over 150 miles away to be found in thin bands around Buxton in Derbyshire, or possibly amongst the very ancient rocks of Charnwood Forest, a 100 miles to the west in Leicestershire. However, the explanation I later learn is both more exotic and more prosaic.

Not many of these small lava blocks have been used to build the church but nevertheless, here they are, weathered and a dull dirty brown. The claim is that they are 'querns', stones used for grinding corn, and that they were recycled by some labour-saving, opportunistic, waste-not-want-not medieval mason. That's the prosaic bit. The exotic strand in the story is that the querns were apparently quarried in Neidermendig in the Eifel region of the Rhineland, Germany. The Neidermendig volcanic lavas made good quality grinding stones and were exported over many centuries to millers all over Europe including, seemingly, the millers around Colney and the surrounding villages.

I'm beginning to think that is quite enough excitement for one day, but I calm down. I climb back on my bike, still following the river, and head off for my final visit on this short trip. The church of St Mary and St Walstan, Bawburgh sits on rising ground just above the River Yare. Its cute round flint tower is capped by a hat of red tiles.

Walstan, the saint, was born in the late 9th century, possibly in Bawburgh, and died in 1016. As a child he received advice and instruction from Bishop Theodred of North Elmham. Although Walstan came from a noble family, aged twelve he renounced worldly-wealth, left home and worked for the rest of his days as a humble farm labourer. His life became one of piety, charity and kindness. He saw angels. And when his body was being returned to Bawburgh for burial, each time the oxen pulling the funeral cart stopped, springs of water miraculously appeared in the ground from which the beasts might drink. The well at Bawburgh is still here. Matching the roofs of the tower and nave, the little well is topped by a covering of red pantiles. Each year pilgrims journey to the well, keen to drink the waters. Not surprisingly, St Walstan became the patron saint of farm workers, farmers and their animals. I take a quick drink, not from the well, but my bottle of water and cycle the seven miles back home.

Norfolk, particularly east Norfolk, has always been good farming country. Even in late Saxon times, settlements were numerous and dense. And wherever you had thriving farmers and tradesmen, you would find a church. While the Saxons tended to be builders in wood, the Normans were builders in stone. For the Normans, stone meant power. Not long after their conquest, the Normans began building new churches, some replacing wooden Saxon ones, some extending those of ruder stone. The bigger and better buildings reflected the new found wealth and industry of the county and its parishes. In fact, as the Normans sought to assert, dominate and control the Anglo-Saxon population, construction began to take place on an epic scale – abbeys, churches, cathedrals, castles.

A couple of centuries after 1066, Norfolk boasted 928 separate parish churches. The Domesday Book, for example, records that in 1066 Norwich alone had 24 churches. By 1086 it had 46, and a castle too. And ten years later, Bishop Herbert Losinga authorised work to begin building Norwich Cathedral. Today, Norwich still claims to have more medieval churches than any other city in Europe.

You are hard pressed as you walk about eastern parts of Norfolk to be out of sight of a church tower, spire or steeple. They rise poetically above the tree line. They seek the higher ground. Protective and mother-like, they are often surrounded by bustling muddles of houses and streets. Just as Norwich city boasts the great number of its churches so Norfolk claims to have more churches than any other county. Although some are no longer in use, an estimated 650 still remain standing.

Many of the first churches to appear were built with the round towers of flint that I have been meeting on my bike ride. And so here, again, is yet another boast. Norfolk claims more round towered churches than any other county – around 120 have been identified, compared to 41 in neighbouring Suffolk, 8 in Essex, and only 12 in the rest of the country.

Most of Norfolk's round towers were built between 1015 and 1115. The fact that some were founded in the years prior to the arrival of the Normans suggests that their design is Saxon in origin. If flint was beginning to replace wood, and if wooden churches were likely to have circular timbered turrets and steeples, then the Saxon craftsmen might well carry on building in the round. The Normans continued to use local craftsmen to build and design many of their churches, especially in the smaller, less wealthy parishes.

But why build towers round rather than square? Maybe local stonemasons couldn't manage square corners when building in flint? Flint is difficult to work and shape. It comes in small pebbles and nodules. Perhaps building circles was easier. However, that explanation seems unlikely, even a little patronising.

The more likely explanation taps into the cultural and historical roots of Saxon Norfolk. The ancestors of many 11th and 12th century Norfolk men and women hailed from northern Germany, a region we know today as Schleswig-Holstein. It is a neck of land that lies immediately south of modern day Denmark. Kiel is its largest city. The eastern shores of Schleswig-Holstein face the Baltic Sea while its western coastline borders the North Sea. Norfolk lies 500 miles to the south south west. It was this 500 mile stretch of sea that the Saxon invaders crossed to settle in Norfolk in the centuries after the Romans left Britain in the year 410.

As the Angles and Saxons made Norfolk their home, trade and cultural links continued between East Anglia and Schleswig-Holstein. And one of the traditions found in this north German region was building towers that were round. Norfolk's round towered churches probably owe their inspiration to the traditions and folk memories of the early medieval builders and their Saxon heritage.

As the county grew richer and more populated, so more and more churches were built. By the 13th, 14th and 15th centuries, more land was being dedicated to sheep rearing and wool production. Wool was highly profitable, and as a result the large estate holders, most of whom had Norman ancestry, became very wealthy.

One way to display your wealth was to support the building of a bigger and better church, a church that was increasingly elaborate and expensively furnished. Freestone, especially limestone, imported from the best quarries in England and France, began to replace some of the flint. Towers became square rather than round. The limestone could be used to support corners, windows and doorways. It could be carved into patterns, decorations and statues. Windows could become larger and more ornate.

Such peacock behaviour resulted in a large number of churches which were grand in scale as well as lovely to look at. White limestone set against the glassy greys and blacks of flint is particularly striking. As you approach these towers of white and shiny black and look up, you have a strong a sense of the power and strength, belief and confidence of those who built and paid for these places of worship, although whether all this brio was by way of thanks to God or a display of conspicuous consumption to impress the neighbours is less clear.

Even today it is a surprise to see so many large, elaborate medieval churches dominating Norfolk's towns and villages. The settlements look far too small to support such grand designs. However, in recognition of the fact that most were built on the profitable backs of medieval sheep, they are now described as 'wool' churches.

One of the cloths woven from the wool was worsted. It takes its name from the village of Worstead twelve miles north east of Norwich. Worsted is a coarse cloth. Its manufacture flourished as weavers from Flanders were encouraged to settle in the county, partly helped by King Edward III's marriage in 1328 to the Flemish princess, Philippa.

Like the landowners who owned the sheep, the weavers of the wool also prospered. And like many of their fellow weavers elsewhere in the county, the Worstead weavers helped pay for a church that would reflect their wealth, status and faith. The church of St Mary, Worstead was begun in the early 14th century and completed in the 15th century in the perpendicular style. It is built on a majestic scale of flint and limestone flushes.

The last Worstead weaver, one John Cubitt, died in 1882, and the village wove no more, at least commercially. There is, however, an annual festival that still takes place in which wool spinning and weaving demonstrations are given, another example of Britain's once great manufacturing base reduced to a heritage industry.

So, from late Saxon times through until the 16th and 17th centuries, based on its farming and agriculture, wool and weaving, Norfolk was a prosperous county with rich families, many of whom could trace their ancestry back to the Normans and their conquest. These families were big land owners. They ran the estates. They supported fine churches, and they built themselves grand houses.

Hugh de Gournay was one of the noblemen who arrived in England with William the Conqueror. Along with many other French knights and noblemen who had helped William conquer England, Hugh was granted extensive lands, in his case stretching across large parts of Norfolk and Suffolk. Over the centuries, descendents of the nobleman continued to live and prosper in East Anglia.

In 1667, one of these descendents, John Gurney, now a Quaker, left his native Essex to work in Norwich. He entered the busy and lucrative woollen trade where, over the years, he made a lot of money. He also married, had eight children, and died in 1721, aged 66. Two of his sons, John and Henry, joined their father in his business, and in turn, two of the younger John's sons, yet another John and another Henry, also entered the trade.

It was this third generation - John (1719-1779) and Henry (1721-1777) - who expanded the business to include banking. And so it was, in 1770 the brothers established Gurney's Bank in Norwich on what is now Pitt Street. By the time the fourth generation of the Norwich Gurneys – Bartlett Gurney – was in charge, the bank had not only grown in size, it had moved to Bank Plain, immediately below the castle.

Being Quakers, the Gurneys were seen as honest and trustworthy. Their bank was regarded as a safe place to keep money and do business. As the years went by, new generations of Gurney men joined the firm and ran the bank. This steady state of affairs continued until the end of the 19th century. And then in 1896 eleven banks, included Gurney's Bank of Norwich, all run by Quaker families, amalgamated. The new bank, with its headquarters in London, became known as Barclays Bank, now, of course, one of the world's leading financial institutions.

The wool trade and banking business had made the Gurneys very rich. In the late 18th century, the family moved to Earlham Hall on the banks of the River Yare on the western fringes of Norwich. The Hall had originally been built in 1642 by Robert Houghton, but over the years extensions and improvements had made it an even more desirable residence. Over the next hundred years, several more generations of Gurneys would be born and brought up at the Hall.

Although she was actually born in Gurney Court, off Magdelen Street in Norwich, one notable Gurney who spent most of her childhood in the family home at Earlham Hall was Elizabeth Fry. She was born in 1780, the daughter of John Gurney (1749-1809) and Catherine whose own mother was a member of the Barclay family, one of the other banking dynasties based in London.

Typical of many wealthy Quakers and their social consciences, Elizabeth became a Christian philanthropist. She married Joseph Fry (yet another banker). They moved to London and had eleven children. But aged 28, she feared her life as a woman was already fated and sealed. Reflecting the feelings of many women down the ages, she wrote in her diary:

My course has been very different to what I had

expected: instead of being, as I had hoped, a useful instrument in the Church Militant, here I am, a care-worn wife and mother…

However, having made that entry, Elizabeth, or Betsy as she was known, found another well of courage and strength. She decided to make her life one that was worthwhile and worth living.

She began this new life as a social reformer. Having been given life, it is up to us to give meaning to it. This, coupled with her Christian faith, was Elizabeth's philosophy. A meaningful life is one that is valued by the person living that life. It must be a morally good life. Living in East London, the first thing in which Elizabeth became interested was the plight of the desperate and poor, particularly those who found themselves in prison.

It was as a prison reformer that she is best remembered. Prisons were places of sickness, hunger, disease and despair. The condition of women prisoners with young children particularly troubled her. As well as campaign for reforms and improvements, she helped set up a school for children and young offenders. She organised classes for women in the belief that education could improve their chances of leading more productive and wholesome lives once they left prison. She set about organising night shelters for the homeless. But the list of her remarkable achievements didn't stop there.

She worried about the loneliness of coastguards and thought that reading books might help. By 1836 she had ensured that all coastguard stations and naval hospitals had small libraries. Along with her younger brother, Joseph John Gurney, she visited prisons and asylums in Britain, Ireland and France. Together, brother and sister campaigned against capital punishment. Elizabeth wrote a book about women and the need to reform prisons. Queen Victoria was a fan and granted Betsy a number of audiences as well as financial support. In 1840 Mrs Fry attended the World Anti-Slavery convention at Exeter Hall in London.

In that same year, along with others, she became involved in setting up a training school for nurses which Florence Nightingale, some years later, visited to recruit trained young women to take with her to the Crimea. We might mention in passing that Nightingale beat Fry to become the first woman to be pictured on a £5 note. Florence's figure and face appeared on all new notes in 1975 before disappearing again in 1994. Elizabeth Fry first featured on the same notes in May 2002. Her portrait appears on the right hand side of the note while on the left-hand side she is depicted reading to prisoners in Newgate prison. Ten years later her image was replaced by that of Winston Churchill.

Elizabeth died in Ramsgate on 12 October 1845. Over a thousand people attended her burial service.

Another good friend of the Gurney family, including Elizabeth but especially her brother Joseph John, was Amelia Opie, née Alderson. She was born in 1769 in a house on Colegate, Norwich, the daughter of Amelia and Dr James Alderson. Her father, a committed member of the Unitarian Church, was one of the first surgeons to work at the newly founded Norfolk and Norwich Hospital sited just outside St Stephens Gate. The hospital was to provide free medical care for the 'deserving poor' and received its first out-patients in 1772. John Anderson was also the family doctor for, as well as a friend of the Gurney family.

In some ways, Amelia's story is even more extraordinary than that of her friend, Elizabeth Fry. From the outset, Amelia set about life with energy and enthusiasm. Rare for an 18th century woman, she quickly became author of her own destiny. She was quick to give her life colour, shape and plenty of content.

There was certainly a strong element of the radical and proto-feminist running through all that Amelia did, and she did a lot. Her early life divided between Norwich and London where she met and mixed with many of the day's more radical artists and literary figures including Walter Scott, William Wordsworth, the poet and playwright Richard Brinsley Sheridan, the actress Sarah Siddons, and the journalist and political philosopher, William Godwin.

Godwin went on to marry the writer and early feminist Mary Wollstonecroft. While she was pregnant, Mary had her portrait painted by the successful Cornish artist, John Opie. The painting, now owned by the National Portrait Gallery, London, shows Mary in a plain, high waisted white gown. She is wearing a soft, black cap. On 30 August 1797, a few months after the picture was finished, Mary gave birth to a baby daughter, also named Mary. But tragedy was to follow.

Only eleven days after the baby's birth, Mary Wollstonecroft died of septicaemia. The child, who would later go on to marry Percy Bysshe Shelley, was raised by her father, William Godwin. Amelia maintained her friendship with William Godwin and kept up her social life with the free-thinking, liberal-minded men and women of North London. Even in such sparkling and radical company, Amelia began to acquire a reputation as a bright, witty, clever conversationalist.

In 1798 she married John Opie, the man who had painted the pregnant Mary's picture. Opie was famed for his portraits and his interpretation of historical subjects. It was while her husband painted that Amelia wrote – letters, songs, poems, plays and novels, including *The Father and Daughter*. Her most successful novel, *Adeline Mowbray*, was published in 1804. The book explored a range of feminist issues – women's education, what today we might call gender politics, society's censorious views about women cohabiting outside marriage, the vulnerability of married women, the search for equality in marriage, and the relationship between mothers and their daughters.

Adeline Mowbray was based on the inspiring but tragic life of her feminist friend, Mary Wollstonecroft. In a bereavement letter to her husband William Godwin, Amelia described Mary approvingly as 'a woman who nobly, and incomparably fought for the violated right of her sex'. Amelia concluded that late 18th and early 19th century society rarely forgave women who transgressed social norms, and with her radical writings and unconventional lifestyle, Mary Wollstonecroft had fallen well short of Georgian society's suffocating standards.

After her husband, John, died in 1807, Amelia moved back to her father's house in Colegate, Norwich. In 1825, and to many people's surprise, aged fifty-six, this energetic, society-loving woman gave up her life as a novelist and socialite and became a Quaker. Her long-standing friendship with the Gurney family – Quakers all – undoubtedly influenced her decision. She dressed more soberly, often in grey. Her interest in philanthropic and charitable works increased. She bought a Georgian house that looked out onto the city's Norman castle, a view of which she said she never tired. The property was sited on the corner of Castle Meadow and a narrow, short thoroughfare that falls away from the castle mound, a road that now bears her name, Opie Street.

I'm on my bike again. I've cycled into Norwich city centre and locked the bike to a rack by the market place. After a short walk along London Street, I'm on Opie Street. I look up, knowing what I shall see. Perched precariously on the parapet above the Café Gelato selling Italian ice-creams and coffees is a small artificial stone statue of Amelia. (See *Plate 13*) Its position appears both odd and unexpected, but there she is. The figurine was commissioned by the Leicester Permanent Building Society which occupied the premises in 1956. And just a few yards further up the street, placed seven or eight feet above the pavement on the wall, not far from where her old house stood on the corner of Opie Street and Castle Meadow, is a square stone plaque, the beginning of which declares:

> Amelia Opie
> Authoress, Dramatist, Poetess
> and brilliant conversationalist

In spite of giving up her London literary life, Amelia's radical instincts remained strong. It's just that they began to express themselves more practically. She remained sympathetic to the rights of women. She argued for equality. She began to immerse herself in works of philanthropy. Her voluntary work included visiting prisons, hospitals, workhouses, the homes of the poor, and refuges for prostitutes. She was an active supporter of the anti-slavery movement and joined Elizabeth Fry at the 1840 World Anti-Slavery Convention in London.

Many years later, not long after returning from a visit to Cromer, her favourite seaside resort where she liked to take a swim, Amelia caught a cold. She became bed-ridden. A year later, in 1853, she died, aged eighty five.

Throughout her later years, Amelia continued to receive a wide variety of friends and acquaintances at her home on Castle Meadow. One young visitor, Harriet Martineau (1802-1876), was born in the same house, Gurney Court off Magdelen Street, Norwich, in which Amelia's friend, Elizabeth Fry had been born twenty two years earlier.

Though a generation younger than Elizabeth and Amelia, Harriet was also a woman of advanced, dissenting and radical views. She was one of the first women to become a journalist. She wrote about the need for social reform, the political economy, social theory and the inequalities suffered by women in a male dominated society. Today, Harriett's reputation is experiencing something of a revival. She is seen by many, including Anthony Giddens, Emeritus Professor of Sociology at the L.S.E., as the first female sociologist, indeed one of the founders of the discipline itself. She is also the subject of an annual lecture – The Harriet Martineau Lecture – which in 2013 was given by the author Ali Smith, in 2014 by the writer Kate Mosse, in 2015 by the political journalist Masha Gessen, and in 2016 by the reggae poet Linton Kwesi Johnson in recognition of Harriet's progressive campaigning on behalf of black emancipation.

However, one of the more unlikely people to visit Amelia in her Castle Meadow home was George Borrow. He was thirty-three years Amelia's junior but as we have seen, an equally colourful, free-ranging spirit.

Amelia had particularly enjoyed reading Borrow's book *The Bible in Spain*, published in 1843. In its day it was an extraordinarily popular book, selling tens of thousands of copies. The hero of the story, Don Jorge, is, of course George Borrow himself. 'Long Live Don Jorge!' writes Amelia cited in Ann Farrant's biography. 'He is my delight both night and morning, and my happiest hours are spent in his society.' I suspect when they met, the two of them got on rather well together.

George and Amelia also shared a Gurney connection. As a boy, George Borrow was inclined to wander the grounds of Earlham Hall, the Gurney's riverside home on the outskirts of Norwich. George would fish in the Yare, true to form, illegally. On one occasion, presumably in the early years of the 19th century, George claimed to have been caught by Elizabeth Fry's older brother and Amelia's friend, Joseph John Gurney who, rather than punish the poacher, invited him to visit the Hall and see the library. Upon questioning the boy about his knowledge of the Scriptures, Joseph John learned that the precocious George could read Greek but not Hebrew. So Joseph John, the Quaker, suggested:

'Thou shouldst study it. Why does thou not undertake the study?'

'I have no books.'

'I will lend thee books, if thou wish to undertake the study.

I live yonder at the hall, as perhaps though knowest. I have a library there, in which are many curious books, both in Greek and Hebrew, which I will show to thee, whenever thou mayest find it convenient to come and see me. Farewell! I am glad to find that thou hast other pursuits more satisfactory than the cruel fishing!'

Elsewhere in his extravagant autobiography, *Lavengro*, George Borrow clearly remembers Earlham Hall and its grounds with some fondness:

On the right side is a green level, a smiling meadow, grass of the richest decks the side of the slope, mighty trees adorn it, giant elms, the nearest of which, when the sun is nigh in its meridian, fling a broad shadow upon the face of the ancient brick of an old English Hall. It has a stately look, that old building, indistinctly seen, as it is, among the umbrageous trees…

Still there with its sweep of green lawns down to the River Yare, Earlham Hall is now part of the University of East Anglia. The refurbished Hall provides a venerable home for the University's School of Law though sadly not its department of business studies, known as the Norwich Business School. It would have been fitting for future men and women of business to find themselves studying in the old home of the Gurneys.

In the case of the business savvy Gurneys, land and wool had led to money and mammon, morally tempered by their Quakerism. However, in the case of another of Norfolk's ancient families, land and wool took them in a different direction – to politics and power.

We have already met them, albeit briefly and at a glance when we learned that Horatio Nelson's maternal great grandmother was Mary Walpole and that Nelson himself was named after his family's benefactor, Horatio Walpole.

Like most of the land-owning elite of the county, the Walpole family traced its roots back to the Normans. By the 13th century the Walpoles had established themselves as respectable men of business. The family continued to be prosperous but remained undistinguished until the 17th century when Sir Edward Walpole, who was a Member of Parliament for King's Lynn, became a Knight of the Order of the Bath.

After Sir Edward's premature death, his son, Robert, took over the family estate. This Robert, known as Colonel Walpole from the rank he held in the Norfolk militia was seen as clever and scholarly, organised and orderly, industrious and ambitious. He was an early advocate of the new ways of farming, including the idea of rotating crops so as not to exhaust the soil. As a result, he began to see his crop yields increase. By the 1670s, his estates were turning in a useful profit, especially from growing turnips, the grazing of sheep and the production of wool.

He frowned upon the old, inefficient ways of farming and, like his fellow land owners, he was happy to enclose what had previously been common land for his own production. As his fortune grew, he bought more estates at nearby Dersingham and West Winch. He also continued the family tradition of being active in politics.

Robert senior's second eldest son, also named Robert, was born on 26 August 1676 in the old manor house at Houghton. Being the younger son, Robert was destined for the church. As a young boy, he was sent, along with his junior brother Horace (Horatio), to a small school at Great Dunham before being packed off to Eton at the age of twelve (although the college was told he was thirteen so that he would qualify as a King's Scholar). At eighteen, Robert went up to King's College, Cambridge. It was while at university that his older brother, Edward, died. This led to a quick and distinct change in the direction of Robert's career and ultimately his fortunes.

Although sympathetic to learning and scholarship, Robert's father was growing frail. After the death of his eldest son, the aging father needed Robert to learn about farming and to manage the large estates as quickly as possible. Robert junior therefore had no choice but to leave Cambridge before completing his studies. By the age of twenty four, the young man was married to Catherine Shotter, the daughter of a rich and successful Kent family. Very shortly after their marriage, in 1770 Robert senior died, aged just fifty.

Immediately after his father's death, Robert threw himself vigorously into farming, a reform of the estates, his marriage, and most crucially, politics. In 1701 he won the parliamentary seat for Castle Rising, just a few miles west of the family home. However, by 1702 he had switched to the 'pocket borough' of King's Lynn where he remained the Whig member for the rest of his long political career.

Like his father, Robert Walpole was extremely ambitious – especially in politics. The early years of the 18th century were a tumultuous time in British politics which were fought fiercely and often dirtily. At one point, Walpole was accused of corruption and in 1712 actually impeached by the House of Commons. He spent the next six months in the Tower of London.

But resilience, skill and determination saw him return with even greater force in the years after his release. By 1721, he had become First Lord of the Treasury, Chancellor of the Exchequer, *and* Leader of the House of Commons all at the same time. Taken together, these roles meant that in effect Robert Walpole had become the most pre-eminent minister in the land – the *de facto* Prime Minister, the first to be recognised as such in British politics, a position sealed after the departure from the scene in 1730 of his brother-in-law, colleague and political rival, Viscount Townshend – 'Turnip' Townshend, fan of the joys of four-fold crop rotation and grower of turnips.

King George II, well disposed to Walpole, gifted him the house at Number 10 Downing Street, London, for his personal use. However, Walpole accepted it only on condition that it became the official residence of whoever was First Lord of the Treasury which is to say, Prime Minister. Walpole remained Prime Minister until 1742. King George II elevated him to the House of Lords where he took the title Earl of Orford.

Throughout his career, Walpole amassed a great fortune. His social, cultural and architectural ambitions were as big as his political ones. The small manor house at Houghton, not far from King's Lynn, where he had been born and raised had been in poor condition when he inherited it from his father. So, feeling the need to live in a house that befitted his status and considerable achievements, Walpole set about building himself a new house on the site of the old family home.

Begun in 1721, it was to be a grand affair built in the Palladian style, quite the fashion of its day. The magnificent silvery-white Yorkshire sandstone mansion, more or less completed by 1730, would become known as Houghton Hall, set in a thousand acres of parkland. To ensure that there were no unwelcome or unsightly views of either unwanted people or ugly houses, the small village of Houghton itself was demolished and the hapless inhabitants relocated to a freshly built New Houghton, round the corner and out of sight.

Walpole was also an enthusiastic collector of paintings and works of art. In its earliest days, Houghton Hall was able to display paintings by Rubens, van Dyck, Rembrandt and Poussin. However, Robert Walpole's grandson, George, who eventually inherited the Hall, was extravagant and feckless and ran up many debts. To help pay for these, in 1779 George, now heir and owner of the Hall, sold most of the works of art – 206 in all – to Catherine the Great of Russia.

A hundred and fifty years later, after the Bolsheviks executed Nicholas II and other members of the Russian royal family, the

Soviet state acquired the paintings. They are on display in the Hermitage Museum, St. Petersburg. But just to show that today there are no hard feelings, in 2014, the Hermitage lent Houghton Hall 70 pieces from the collection. For several glorious months, many of the paintings by van Dyck, Rembrandt and many others once more found themselves hanging on the walls in their original places as part of a remarkable exhibition organised by the Hall's present owners, the Cholmondeleys, something of a diplomatic as well as cultural coup.

On the death in 1797 of the 4th Earl of Orford, Horatio, *aka* Horace Walpole (youngest son of Robert Walpole, the Prime Minister, and cousin of Nelson's maternal grandmother, and after whom, as we learned earlier, Nelson was named), the Hall was inherited by Robert Walpole's daughter Mary. Mary was married to George Cholmondeley, 3rd Earl of Cholmondeley. She therefore became Lady Cholmondeley. Houghton Hall has remained in the possession of the Cholmondeley/Walpole family ever since.

Today, the Hall is the home of David Cholmondeley, 7th Marquess of Cholmondeley and his wife Rose. Their next door neighbour – well, the neighbour who lives on the nearby estate five miles down the road, is the Queen, at least when she is staying at her Norfolk home, Sandringham House with its two pretty gatehouses made of brown gingerbread carstone.

However, on a more unsettling note, the continued presence of so many land-owning families able to trace their privilege and ancestry back to the 11th and 12th centuries troubled some of Norfolk's more radical souls of which, over the years, there have been a fair number, as we shall see.

Chapter 11
Rascals and Radicals

Put rather crudely, since Norman times, a small number of elite families have continued to own much of Norfolk, indeed much of England. From the moment of their arrival in the late 11th century, the Norman invaders set about dispossessing the native English of their lands. They ruled with military might, rigour and ruthlessness. And in the space of few decades, the Normans and their cronies had all but replaced the old English Anglo-Saxon elite. These Norman autocrats spoke old French. It would be several hundred years before the kings of England spoke English as their first language. It is therefore no surprise to learn that this new conquering gentry and their descendents rapidly became entrenched, powerful and rich.

As we have seen, Norfolk was then, and remains good farming country. The land was still worked by the English, but their station in life had fallen dramatically. They had become peasants. They were wage-earning serfs, villeins, or at best free common men and tenant farmers. They now found themselves at the bottom of a feudal hierarchy. Placed above them with increasing power and wealth were the lords, squires and knights; the barons, earls and dukes; and finally the king with whom ultimate power and authority rested.

Recent genetic evidence suggests that the ancestors of this medieval peasant population were mainly a mixture of Pre-Roman Britons and North German Anglo-Saxons. Even in modern south and east England, researchers find surprisingly little Roman, Viking or Norman DNA in the genetic make-up of the majority of the current native population suggesting that the economic and political elites did not, and maybe still don't fraternise, never mind breed overly much with the old English peasantry with their Anglo-Saxon and ancient British pedigree.

In feudal societies it was the peasants who got their hands dirty. They produced the wool and wheat, the barley and oats, and the turnips and swedes which helped make the fortunes of the land owners and landlords. In later centuries, as their wealth continued to grow, the richest and most powerful of these land-owning families built many of Norfolk's most stately of homes – Felbrigg Hall, Blickling Hall, Holkham Hall, Houghton Hall, Oxburgh Hall and Wolterton Hall.

Not surprisingly the peasant population made up of an integrated mix of ancient Britons, Anglo-Saxons and a sprinkling of Vikings was not entirely happy with their new feudal lot. But on the whole there was little they could do about it. The Normans were too strong, too organised and too smart to be worried by the thought that the natives might get restless. Their confidence was visibly and symbolically expressed in stone – soaring cathedrals, countless churches, impregnable castles, and grand houses.

Of course, from time to time the peasants felt hard done by and they did revolt. In 1381, Wat Tyler led a rebellion down in Kent. Increasingly heavy levies in the form of a poll tax to fund the inefficiencies and extravagances of the royal court was a major grievance. The number of people who still lived as unfree serfs also continued to be a source of discontent.

This Peasants' Revolt quickly spread across much of south east England. Tyler and his men entered London, killing a number of powerful establishment figures including the Lord Chancellor. However, within a few months, King Richard II, also known as Richard of Bordeaux, and his men managed to quash the Great Rising, and by the summer of that year, Tyler had been killed.

The revolt, though, had also spread into East Anglia. In Norfolk, Geoffrey Litester (sometimes spelled Litster or Lister), a weaver and dyer from the hamlet of Felmingham west of North Walsham, had gathered the support of many of his fellow men. The angry band marched on Norwich and assembled outside the city on 17 June 1381. The city's governor, Sir Robert Salle, himself of relatively humble origins, rode out to meet the rebels hoping to negotiate a peaceful resolution. The talks didn't go well. Clearly not a gifted diplomat, the knight managed to enrage the men even further. A skirmish took place and Sir Robert was killed.

The city gates were opened. The rebels briefly captured and then took over the city of Norwich before finally retreating to a heath near North Walsham. Violence quickly spread across the county as the deep resentments that had been building up over many years led to attacks on property, official records and foreigners.

In London and the counties, one by one the various uprisings had been put down, ruthlessly and often brutally. The very last rebellion to be dealt with in the country concluded with the Battle of North Walsham, fought in late June 1381 between the Norfolk rebels and the forces of the church and state. North Walsham is a Norfolk town founded in Anglo-Saxon times. It had gained much of its medieval size and prosperity from the wool and weaving industry.

The Bishop of Norwich at the time, Henry le Despenser, was of French noble stock. In spite of being a senior figure in the clergy, it was the Bishop who decided to take on the rebels. With a heavily armed force, he marched north to the market town. It helps to know that prior to being a bishop, Despencer had been a soldier in Italy. This led to his soubriquet, the 'Fighting Bishop.'

Geoffrey Litester also had a soubriquet: 'The King of the Commons'. But he was soon captured by the bishop and his men. The clergyman's successful efforts defeating the peasants earned this excitable, somewhat bloodthirsty account by the medieval chronicler, Thomas Walsingham:

> The warlike priest, like a wild boar gnashing its teeth, spared neither himself nor his enemies, stabbing one

man, knocking down another and wounding a third. Nor did he cease his violent struggles until the whole crowd which fell on him when he reached the ditch were ready to fly.

For his treachery, Geoffrey Litester was condemned to death. But Walsingham, the anti-rebel chronicler, goes on to add that Henry le Despencer, being a Christian and merciful man, decided to hear Litester's confession. And then, being a compassionate man, held the rebel's head as he was being dragged to the gallows to save it being knocked and bruised as he was hauled along the ground. After this supposed act of Christian kindness, Litester was then hung, drawn and quartered. One quarter of his body was sent to Norwich, one to Great Yarmouth, another to King's Lynn, and the remainder was exhibited outside Litester's house in Felmingham 'so that rebels, and those who rise against the peace, may learn how it will end.'

Nevertheless, having dispatched the rebel leader, the bishop remained nervous about his safety. It was le Despencer, remember, who converted Herbert de Losinga's old chapel at North Elmham, the sight of Norfolk's wooden Anglo-Saxon cathedral, into a fortified, turreted manor house. This became the place of safety to which he would retreat whenever there was a hint of trouble.

And so ended The Peasants' Revolt. Today, the remains of three stone crosses commemorate the Battle of North Walsham. The easiest one to spot, standing ten foot high, is by the side of the Norwich Road near Toff's Loke, a few hundred yards to the east of where the battle took place, and less than a mile south of North Walsham town centre. For stone cross enthusiasts, Grid Reference TG 2783 2828 is the place to go and find it.

Modern minds seem more sympathetic to the peasants and their revolt. We have already met the artist and carver of massive tree trunks, Mark Goldsworthy of Bungay. It was Mark who chiselled and chipped a tribute to Will Kemp, the marathon morris man and his wondrous nine-day dance to Norwich. But he has also sculpted a wonderful piece to commemorate the Peasants' Revolt and the Battle of North Walsham along with the Agricultural Workers Union which was fittingly founded in North Walsham in 1906. Standing massive and tall, the figures carved in oak climb fifteen feet high. The sculpted piece, unveiled in 1999, can be found in the park next to the Memorial Gardens in the centre of North Walsham.

However, at the time of the revolt, there was little sympathy felt by the privileged classes for the labouring men and women of England. This was a time when you were born into your divinely ordained station in life. You were expected to know your place. King Richard II, who had negotiated with Wat Tyler, reneged on his promise to free the serfs, allegedly saying 'rustics you were and rustics you are still. You will remain in bondage, not as before, but incomparably harsher.' No one-nation sympathies there.

I like to think that throughout the ages, rebellious hearts have beaten away in the bosoms of Norfolk's flinty men and spirited women. We saw rebellion erupt in magnificent fury in the breast of the county's Celtic warrior, Boudica, Queen of the Iceni when she took on the duplicitous Romans. Geoffrey Litester and his brothers challenged the feudal hierarchy that kept the lords of the manor in money and power. And 168 years later, another Norfolk man, Robert Kett, decided he had had enough of feeling trampled and tricked by the county's big landowners. But first, let's go back a while and take an even longer view of the relationship between those who toil and the land upon which they live.

At the end of the last Ice Age, some 10,000 years ago and before people took up farming, small kinship groups roamed the open lands of what is now the southern North Sea basin, that which we now call Doggerland. As we learned in earlier chapters, Norfolk was part of the western fringes of these post-glacial river plains. The land was rich in both plant and wild life. These Stone Age, Mesolithic families were hunters and gatherers. There were no boundaries. No-one owned the land. The very idea would have seemed alien and odd.

By Neolithic times, 5 or 6,000 years ago, people were beginning to settle and take up a farming life. Even so, much of the land was held in common, that is, the fields were open and the land was shared. Any man's pigs could root in the woods. People could wander into the forests and gather wood for fuel or fell timber for housing. Game could be hunted by anyone who had the skill, time and energy. The fish were there for the taking. The notion that the land could be held exclusively by a private individual would have been difficult to understand.

The idea of the common land on which crops could be grown and cattle grazed remained the shared belief for several thousand years until the arrival of the Normans. Then things began to change rapidly. Throughout the 12th and 13th centuries, the invaders and their kings began to claim land as exclusively theirs, privately owned and out of bounds to the masses.

One of the provisions of the Statute of Merton, enacted in 1235, allowed Lords of the Manor to enclose, that is fence off and privatise what had previously been common, communal land, so long as tenants had sufficient left to be able to feed and support themselves. The Statute became the basis of English common law in which the idea that land could be legally owned by an individual became statute.

However, it was not until the 15th and 16th centuries that the rich and powerful seriously began to set about increasing the size of their estates. More and more land was enclosed and privatised. The open field system of feudal England slowly disappeared as the great landowners claimed more and more of the countryside as belonging to them.

In part, The Peasant's Revolt of 1381 had been against the state wanting to simplify the idea of who owned the land and determine how it should be used. For those in power, the idea of common ownership was too vague and inefficient. The common lands had been used in many ways for all kinds of purpose – pasture, arable, foraging, and hunting. Hay could be gathered. Pigs could be left to gorge on autumn acorns. Lakes and rivers could be fished. But the rich and powerful rationalised their greed by alleging that traditional common land practices were too piecemeal and lacked discipline. They pushed for each piece of common land to be owned by just one person.

In many parts of the country, including Norfolk, raising sheep was one of the lures and incentives to appropriate and enclose what had previously been a communal resource. Sheep produced wool, and wool and weaving were becoming very profitable. And so with the support of further legislation, those who already had land and power, grabbed even more. It was only when some men had successfully claimed ownership of the flowing rivers and the grassy fields, the dense forests and open woods, that catching fish and trapping rabbits, hunting deer and shooting birds became a crime – the crime of poaching – if the land was no longer yours.

Many of the more brazen land grabs triggered anger and outrage in the hearts and minds of small-scale farmers and tenants. The farmers and peasants were left with less and less common land on which to graze their animals, trap their supper, collect their wood and fell their timber.

For so long, the idea that the earth could be privately owned by individuals had seemed alien, indeed sacrilegious to those whose lives were most intimately connected with the earth and its waters. The hunters and gatherers, farmers and woodsmen felt that the land affected them every bit as much as they affected the land. The itinerant priest, John Ball, who had played a prominent role in the Peasants' Revolt of 1381, famously began one of his open-air sermons with that most radical, most egalitarian of questions:

When Adam delved and Eve span, who was then the
gentleman?

And the question has continued to reverberate down the ages.
Even today, a small number of ancient and aristocratic families,
private institutions, and the Crown still own two thirds of the
land in Britain. Working men and women, the land poor, and
the urban classes still have to fight for the right to roam and
ramble over the country's moors and mountains, heathlands
and valleys, river banks and coastal paths.

Sir John Flowerdew was a Norfolk lawyer and landowner.
He lived in the village of Hethersett which lies just outside
Norwich. He had supported Henry VIII's drive to dissolve and
destroy the monasteries. It was Sir John who oversaw much
of the dismantling of the monastic buildings associated with
Wymondham Abbey, founded in 1107. As a reward he became
King Henry VIII's local agent. The destructive urges of the agent
were not viewed too well by the locals. So when Sir John went
on to enclose some of the common lands around Hethersett, the
community felt incensed.

On the 6 July 1549, after attending a feast and an illegal
performance of a play honouring the memory of Thomas Becket,
co-patron of Wymondham Abbey, a group of men marched
north east towards Hethersett hell-bent on tearing down Sir
John's freshly planted hedges and newly erected fences.

But Sir John, being a smooth-talking lawyer as well as an
ambitious landowner, parleyed with the rioters. In the event,
tricky words proved insufficient so he simply bribed the men
to leave his fences alone and instead return south west and
pull down those built by the Wymondham farmer and yeoman
tanner, the 57-years-old Robert Kett.

Kett and Flowerdew had history. Kett had been unhappy
about the part that Sir John had played in dismantling parts

of Wymondham Abbey. The farmer was one of those who had helped save that part of the Abbey which functioned as the parish church by raising money and buying it from the crown. However, his efforts had brought him into conflict with Sir John who continued in his attempts to dismantle the Abbey even after the parishioners had paid good money for its protection. It was these conflicts with Kett that motivated the knight to talk the rebels into attacking Kett's enclosures and not his own.

So off marched the rioters, back to Wymondham, where they voiced their grievances to Kett. As it turned out, the good farmer sympathised with their case. In fact, he decided not only to join them but lead them in their cause. And so was born Kett's Rebellion. First, he took down his own fences and returned the land to common use. The rebels then went back to Hethersett and tore down and ripped up Sir John Flowerdew's hedges and fences.

Excited by their daring, the next day on 9 July 1549, the men headed off to Norwich. People from other villages joined them, fuelled by the strong sense of unfairness that the rich and strong were so casually taking from the poor and weak. The protesters met by an oak tree in Hethersett on the road to Norwich. Gathering more and more men, the rebellion continued on its way to the city, looting and plundering as it went.

1549 had been a year of dissatisfaction across many parts of the country. There were risings in Devon and Cornwall, the Midlands and the Thames valley, Essex and Hertfordshire, Suffolk and Cambridgeshire. There was dissatisfaction not only with more and more common land being enclosed and privatised by rich landowners, but also a more general anger felt towards the gentry and the unfettered power they held. The year of risings became known as the 'commotion time'. Disorder was rife. Fences were ripped down. Wine cellars emptied. Poaching became rampant.

Kett's rebellion was relatively late on the scene but proved to be the most violent. In part this was down to the particular mistrust and dislike of the landed gentry by Norfolk's labourers, yeomen and peasants.

On 21 July, the rebels set camp on Mousehold Heath, a tract of high ground overlooking the city. Kett established his headquarters beneath another oak, christened the Oak of Reformation. A Herald of the Crown was sent to meet the rebels. He offered Kett and his men a pardon if they ceased their effronteries and dispersed peacefully. However, his attitude did not go down well with the rebels. They rejected the offer, stormed the gates, and by late July had taken control of the city

Down in London, the increasingly outraged Lord Protector, the Duke of Somerset, then sent Sir William Parr, the Marquis of Northamptonshire, with a small army, to deal with the rebels. At first, Northampton's men had some success. They managed to gain entry into the city, but after a fierce battle at St Martin's in the Plain, Kett recaptured Norwich. The bruised, battered and rather humiliated army of the Marquis of Northampton retreated to Cambridge.

Opposition to the rebels within the city was limited. Many Norwich people were sympathetic to the cause. Nevertheless, a number of aldermen, the mayor and a few of the local gentry were imprisoned. Kett and his men were now back in control.

The fall of Norwich was viewed with grave disquiet by the crown authorities in London. By late August, John Dudley, the Earl of Warwick was dispatched to deal with the upstarts. He arrived with an even larger army of between 8,000 and 12,000 men, some of whom were battle-hardened foreign mercenaries and some of whom were mounted Norfolk landowners 'keen to punish their tenants for their impudence.'

Before engaging in battle, Warwick thought it prudent to try once more to negotiate. He sent his herald to offer a pardon to the rebels if they agreed to disarm. But the offer was not trusted. One of the rebel boys, wishing to show his contempt for the herald, bared his backside to the visitor. Many years later, in 1615, a chronicler by the name of Richard Woods wrote, possibly not entirely reliably, and, according to the historian Andy Wood, certainly not sympathetically, that:

> It happened that, before [the herald] had made an end of his speech, that an ungracious boy, putting down his breeches, shewed his bare buttocks & did a filthy act: adding thereunto more filthy words.

A soldier escorting the herald was so enraged by this rudery that he killed the boy. Kett, who was on the point of going to speak with Warwick, was held back by his angry men who by now saw only lies and treachery on the part of Warwick and his representatives.

The Earl of Warwick had had enough. He lost patience and attacked the city. After several days of fighting, Warwick took Norwich. The rebels who survived re-grouped to the east of the town. But Warwick pursued them. The decisive battle took place on the low valley plains of Dussindale on the eastern outskirts of the city. The fighting was fierce but the rebels were outmanoeuvred and less well equipped. As well as the many men who had been killed in battle, Warwick hanged many more after their defeat.

Robert Kett and his brother William escaped but were soon captured. They were taken to the Tower of London, tried for treason, and found guilty. They were returned to Norwich. On 7 December 1549, Robert was hanged in chains from the battlements of Norwich Castle. William was taken to Wymondham where he was also hanged in chains from the tower of the Abbey. It is said that the brothers took several days to die. Their bodies were left to rot in full public view.

Part of the explanation for the rebels' intransigence and the bloodiness of the fighting was the profound mistrust and ill-feeling between the rural and urban poor on the one hand and the county landowners and the city merchants on the other. The common enemy of the county's labouring men and women was the gentry. The rich had enclosed common land, grown the size of their sheep flocks, increased rents, knocked down the dwellings of the poor to enlarge their own houses, and established private deer parks, all at the expense of the common man. Little wonder that resentment ran dangerous and deep. The 'gents and richemen,' said one rebel, '…have all [the] catell and wolles…in their hands nowe a dayes and the pore peple are now famysshed.'

In the years immediately after the 'commotion', the rebels were dismissed as 'rude and rusticall people' and 'rascals and naughtie lewd persons'. By late 1549, Sir John Cheke was arraigning the 'rabble'. He was Professor of Greek at the University of Cambridge, a member of parliament, and a statesman. He wanted to know by what right the 'commotioners' thought they could attack 'gentlemen'. How dare they.

> Why should you hate them thus? For their riches or for their rule? ... Is this your true duetie…to disobieie your betters, and to obeie your tanners, to change your obedience from the king to a Ket?... In countries some must rule, some must obeie, everie man maie not beare like stroke: for every man is not like wise.

But we live in different times. Today Robert Kett is seen as something of a hero and apologies are offered. A rectangular stone plaque on the walls of Norwich Castle was unveiled in 1949, four hundred years after his execution. The inscription, chiselled in capital letters, reads:

IN 1549 A D ROBERT KETT YEOMAN FARMER OF WYMONDHAM WAS EXECUTED BY HANGING IN THIS CASTLE AFTER THE DEFEAT OF THE NORFOLK REBELLION OF WHICH HE WAS THE LEADER. IN 1949 A D - FOUR HUNDRED YEARS LATER – THIS MEMORIAL

WAS PLACED HERE BY THE CITIZENS OF NORWICH IN REPARATION AND HONOUR TO A NOTABLE AND COURAGEOUS LEADER IN THE LONG STRUGGLE OF THE COMMON PEOPLE OF ENGLAND TO ESCAPE FROM A SERVILE LIFE INTO THE FREEDOM OF JUST CONDITIONS.

Elsewhere we find a bronze roundel relief forged on the bottom right of the centre door of Norwich City Hall. It depicts Robert Kett hanging against the castle walls. Designed by James Woodford, the doors were installed in 1938. (See *Plate 14*)

In Wymondham, we have the Robert Kett Primary School. The school doesn't have a Kett inspired motto. However, it does seek inspiration from another rebel, Nelson Mandela. In large blue letters the school approvingly quotes the South African freedom fighter and leader who said 'Education is the most powerful weapon you can use to change the world.' Kett by name; Mandela in spirit. That's a radical marriage by any standard.

And just half a mile east of the school we find Kett's Park. In one of those nice ironies of geography and history, the park sits next door to the county headquarters of today's law enforcers, the Norfolk Police. Quite what they'd make of a rabble of 'rude and rusticall and naughtie lewd persons' marching out of Wymondham today, I'm not sure.

The B1140, known as Kett's Hill, rises steeply from the River Wensum and skirts the southern flanks of Mousehold Heath where the 16th century protester and his followers had made camp around the Oak of Reformation. This oak has long since disappeared.

However, the other oak in Kett's story still stands, just, with a little help from timber supports. It is the tree on the Wymondham-Hethersett border where the rebels first met before they marched on to Norwich. It is known as Kett's Oak. It lives alone, looking rather forlorn, on the side of the B1172. (See *Plate 15*)

I used to meet a friend in Wymondham. I'd cycle from Norwich and we would go on bike rides together. It's a while since I've cycled to the market town but the morning is bright and mercifully the wind has dropped. It seems a good day to visit the old tree. I must have passed it scores of time but never stopped to take a proper look. So today, rather than rush by, I park my bike on the grass verge. It is not a huge tree. For an ancient oak, it looks rather small, perhaps even a little disappointing. Its old limbs have been patched up with iron bands, tarred felt and even cement. But it has been witness to remarkable events and changing times. The tree is circled by a metal railing. At its base there is a small aluminium plaque that reads:

A Historic View of Kett's Oak.
Kett's Oak, although it stands just inside the Hethersett Parish boundary, is named after Robert and William Kett of Wymondham, who assembled their men at this point in 1549, before marching on Norwich.
Their grievances were mainly to do with enclosing the common lands and the rising cost of living. Various enclosure hedges were 'thrown down' by their respective followers, and the revolt was underway.
The rebellion failed and Robert Kett was hanged at Norwich Castle. His brother William was hanged from the tower of Wymondham Abbey.

I take a photograph. The light is good but a dark cloud is making its way from the west threatening a heavy shower. I toy with the idea of cycling through Wymondham and on to Thetford but age, a possible soaking and failed ambition see me climbing back on my bike and heading home to Norwich. The frisky black cloud catches me anyway and I arrive home wet. But I do need to re-visit Thetford. It's an ancient town that has been home to some remarkable people.

Although born a couple of centuries after Kett and his rebellion, Thomas Paine was yet another Norfolk man who was angered by the arrogance of the gentry and their 'landed interests'. He was born in 1737, in Thetford. The town lies twenty miles further down the London Road from Kett's Wymondham. Seventeen hundred years earlier Queen Boudica had lived in and around the Thetford area. Paine's mother was an Anglican and the daughter of a local lawyer. His father was a Quaker, a stay-maker, and a small holder. The marriage between Establishment Anglicanism and Quaker dissent must have made for an interesting childhood for the young Thomas. He proved to be a bright boy and for five years he was a pupil at Thetford Grammar School.

His early career was chequered. After leaving school, he became an apprentice stay-maker in Thetford, flirted with journalism, went to sea, became a teacher, and had a job as an excise officer. It was while he was in London that he was introduced to the American writer, political theorist, scientist and inventor, Benjamin Franklin, who would go on to be one of America's Founding Fathers. The year was 1774. Franklin encouraged Paine to emigrate to America which he did. With his experience as a writer and journalist, when Tom arrived in his adopted country he took on the job of editing the *Pennsylvania Magazine*.

In 1776, Thomas Paine published his influential and highly readable pamphlet, *Common Sense*. Along with another short tract, the *Free and Independent States of America*, the essay offered powerful support to the idea that the American colony should seek independence from British rule. And indeed, a few months later, on 4 July 1776, the American Declaration of Independence was made.

In the following years, Paine remained an active supporter and sympathiser as America fought its protracted war with Britain for independence. Freedom from British rule was finally achieved in 1783. The *Treaty of Paris* marked the end of the war between the Americans and the British and the sovereignty and independence of the United States was finally recognised.

In the subsequent years, Paine made a number of visits to France, still a monarchy at the time. On one of his visits in 1787, this extraordinary man submitted plans to build a single-arch iron bridge of his own design and invention, another radical idea at the time. In spite of this foray into engineering, his political radicalism continued to grow, and true to form, he became sympathetic to the aims of those French men and women who wished to see more equality, liberty and fairness in their country. He kept faith with his American ideals and continued championing the idea of republican democracies.

In 1789, the Bastille in Paris, the notorious state prison used by the kings of France to incarcerate their dissident citizens, was attacked. This marked the beginning of the French Revolution. Edmund Burke, an Irish political theorist and philosopher, criticised the Revolution, even though he had written previously in support of similar grievances expressed by the American colonists. It was Burke's 1790 essay, *Reflections on the Revolution in France*, which argued in favour of inherited wealth, status and power, that provoked Paine into writing *The Rights of Man*. The book was a vigorous response to Burke's conservatism. Burke favoured tradition and convention. Paine championed the common people and argued for their natural rights.

In his pamphlets and correspondence Paine had expressed sympathy with the aims of the English Peasants' Revolt of 1381. Indeed, much of his writing echoed John Ball's feelings about greed and injustice, privilege and preferment. Ball, the radical priest of the Peasants' Revolt, had written four hundred years earlier that:

> From the beginning all men by nature were created alike, and our bondage and servitude came in by unjust oppression of haughty men… And therefore I exhort you to consider that now the time is come,

appointed to us by God, in which you may (if ye will) cast off the yoke of bondage, and recover liberty.

And here is Paine's in similar mood writing in the late 18th century about the same British landed gentry several centuries later:

The aristocracy are not the farmers who work the land, and raise the produce, but are the mere consumers of the rent; and when compared to the active world are the drones, a seraglio of males, who neither collected the honey nor form the hive, but exist only for lazy enjoyment.

When Paine was a boy, Thetford was in decline. There was a growing divide between rich and poor. The rich loathed the idea of giving up any of their land, wealth or privilege. Even minor crimes by the poor – crimes of theft and poaching – were dealt with harshly, including execution. The number of public hangings increased throughout the 18th century, and the house that Tom Paine lived in as a boy was in sight of Thetford's own place of hanging – Gallow's Hill.

Most regional estate holders were beneficiaries of the various 'Inclosure Acts' that had been placed on statute over the centuries. The Acts granted them legal property rights over land that had previously been open and common to all. One of the biggest landowners in the Thetford area was the Duke of Grafton, Charles FitzRoy, one time Lord Lieutenant of Ireland and Lord Chamberlain – the senior official of the Royal Household, a post which he held until his death in 1757. He lived at Euston Hall, a few miles to the south east of Thetford.

Throughout the 18th and especially the 19th century, more and more land was being enclosed and privatised by the large estate holders. The theft of the fields, hills and open spaces accelerated. Where people were once free to roam, they now found themselves outlawed as trespassers and poachers.

'Inclosure came and trampled the grave, of labour's rights and left the poor a slave' wrote the poet John Clare. Like other major landowners intent on increasing their estates, the second Duke of Grafton felt the view from his home could be improved by knocking down and re-siting the village of Euston. And this he did.

The Graftons held huge powers of patronage. It made them even more politically powerful and financially influential. Their grip on local affairs also encouraged corruption and injustice. Nearly all important offices were in the gift of the Dukes. However, they did have one or two good points. The second Duke was an enthusiastic patron of music and one of the original sponsors of London's Foundling Hospital, a charity for orphaned children.

Nevertheless, it is hard to avoid the conclusion that some of Tom Paine's early radicalism, opposition to injustice and inequality, anti-privilege, and hostility to inherited wealth and status must have been shaped by his awareness of how the lives of the rich were ones of power and opulence, while those of the poor were ones of impotence and desperation. We get a delightful hint of Tom's youthful radicalism in the epitaph he wrote for his pet crow, John, written when he was eight years old.

> Here lies the body of John Crow.
> Who once was high but now is low;
> Ye brother Crows take warning all,
> For as you rise, so must you fall.

Forty six years later in 1791, his radicalism undimmed, Thomas Paine wrote the first volume of *The Rights of Man*, partly in defence of the French Revolution, and partly with the intention of promoting republicanism in England. The second volume was published a year later just as Britain was about to go to war with France. The British government saw Paine's books as seditious, even traitorous. To escape any possible arrest, he moved to Paris. In his absence, the British courts did indeed find him guilty of treason and outlawed him.

Paine remained in post-revolutionary France even though it was a turbulent and unpredictable place. This was the time known as 'The Reign of Terror'. In 1793, Paine crossed swords with Robespierre, a powerful member of the Committee of Public Safety. Upsetting Robespierre was generally a bad move. Paine was accused of being an enemy of the Revolution. This was a crime that almost always led to execution. He was imprisoned in late 1793.

Never one to idle away the hours, over the months in which he was incarcerated, Paine managed to carry on writing. He produced the *Age of Reason*, a book which criticised mainstream Christianity, its institutionalisation, and the power and corruption of the established Church. Although he believed in God, he also argued that men and women should live according to the rational insights produced by human reason rather than order the world based on mythical biblical stories as revealed, interpreted and promoted by clerical scholars and their interests.

In July 1794, still in prison, Paine was scheduled to be executed. But the story goes that his cell had been open when the gaolers went along marking the doors of those prisoners due to be killed the following morning. Paine's door, because it was open, had inadvertently been marked on the inside. The door was then shut for the night and so the mark was no longer visible to anyone passing by the cells. The next morning when the death cart was collecting prisoners for their final journey to the guillotine, the executioners, seeing no white mark, passed Tom's door and left him in his cell.

A few days later, Robespierre himself was executed. Tom Paine remained in prison until his release on 6 November 1794 mainly due to the efforts of the American minister to France, James Munroe, who convinced the authorities that Paine was an

American citizen. Paine stayed on in France. There he continued to write his political essays and express his radical ideas. In one essay, *Agrarian Justice*, he once more railed against the idea that land could or should be privately owned.

Paine's extraordinary and unlikely life continued. In 1800 he met Napoléon Bonaparte, who said that he was a fan of *The Rights of Man*. However, Napoléon's commitment to the rights of men was somewhat spoiled when, in 1804, he proclaimed himself Emperor of France. Even before then, Tom was becoming bothered by Napoléon's increasingly dictatorial tendencies. So in 1802, at the invitation of President Thomas Jefferson, he returned to America, to retire and lead a quieter life. He was 65 years old.

His recent writings and quarrels with a whole host of different people meant that his reception in America was less warm and more muted than it had been in the past. America's growing rich and privileged elite did what the rich and privileged generally do. They became increasingly more conservative, and Paine's views on power, protection, equality and inheritance were becoming less to their taste, even though his ideas had once helped sponsor and fuel the country's fight for independence.

In his late sixties Paine's health began to deteriorate. He died in 1809, aged 72, in what is now Greenwich Village, New York. His truculent, often uncompromising behaviour meant that few bothered to turn up to his funeral and for a while his reputation and role in America's fight for independence went almost forgotten.

As with so many of yesterday's rebels, history has been kind to Thomas Paine too. Today, in America, Britain, France and throughout the world he is recognised as a pioneer of human freedom, human rights, justice and equality. He argued that the idea of inherited land and wealth, concentrated power and privilege were just plain wrong. The notes of his life which introduce the Everyman edition of his book, *The Rights of Man*, conclude:

He had been in his lifetime an embarrassment to those in government; a man of reason who lived by principles, placing the rights of the underprivileged before power and property. (p vii)

Thomas Edison, the famous inventor, went so far as to say he regarded Paine as 'one of the greatest of all Americans'. Many now see Paine and his writings, particularly his essay *Common Sense*, as laying the groundwork for America's declaration of independence and belief in the rights and freedoms of all men and women.

By anybody's standards, Paine's life and achievements are remarkable. He influenced governments. He met many of the great men of the late 18th and early 19th centuries. His books are still in print. Political theorists and social reformers still quote him. Even his design for a single-arch iron bridge was eventually realised, not in France but of all places Sunderland, England. The first bridge over the River Wear was built of iron and was based on Paine's model for a bridge over the Schuykill River in Philadelphia. It opened in 1796 but was later demolished as new bridges were built.

I've taken the train to Thetford to have a wander round the ancient Breckland town. Thetford was rather slow, even reluctant to recognise their famous son. But now, on King Street, there is a coppery-gold coloured statue of Thomas Paine. (See *Plate 16*) It was designed by Sir Charles Wheeler and erected in 1964. Paine is holding a quill pen in one hand and a copy of *The Rights of Man* in the other. The sculptor was possibly inspired by a letter sent to Paine by Thomas Jefferson in June 1793 in which the man destined to become America's third President wrote:

Go on then doing with your pen what in other times was done with the sword; shew that reformation is more practicable by operating on the mind than on the body of man, and be assured that it has not a more sincere votary, nor you a more ardent well-wisher than, Dear Sir, Your friend and servt,

Th. Jefferson

All around the limestone plinth on which the statue stands are quotes from the *Age of Reason*, though none, it has to be said, voicing his anti-monarchist thoughts. Quite what the republican Tom would have made of his statue being sited on King Street, I'm not sure.

There are other commemorations to be found in Thetford town. I take a short walk from his statue to his old school, Thetford Grammar, still going strong. There I read a plaque that mentions he was a pupil at the school from 1744 to 1749. I retrace my steps and head across town to visit The Thomas Paine Hotel. Just outside its main entrance is a neat, round plaque marking the nearby birthplace of their man:

Birthplace of
Thomas Paine
1737 – 1809
Author of 'The Rights of Man'. 'Common Sense'
and 'Age of Reason'. He played an important role in the
French Revolution and also in American Politics.
Paine is regarded as a hero in America, as he was the first
person to call for 'An Independent but United States of
America'.

And to seal that last claim, further along on another wall of the hotel I find a second metal plaque. It was placed and paid for by men of the American Air Force who were based in Norfolk in 1943. Part of the inscription reads "…this simple son of England lives on through the Ideals and Principles of the democratic world for which we fight today."

We've already noted that Thetford's other rebel and one-time resident, Boudica, has a statue cast in her honour opposite the Houses of Parliament. But poor old Geoffrey Litester, leader of the Peasant's Revolt in Norfolk, and killed at the Battle of North Walsham by the fighting Bishop and his men goes almost unrecognised. I am unaware of any plaque or statue that honours his personal memory. But there is a Litester Close in North Walsham, a suburban *cul de sac* lined with bungalows. And that seems to be it.

Robert Kett, as we've seen, has fared much better with his plaques and his bronze door, his oak and school, his park and road all bearing his name. Even better, in 2014, The Woodland Trust named Kett's Oak in Hethersett as one of England's top ten trees. Although it didn't make the number one spot, like the winner, the Major Oak in Sherwood Forest, Kett's Oak has come to symbolise the struggles of the dispossessed against the greed and wealth of the landed gentry. The Major Oak was the alleged hiding place of Robin Hood and his men. Robin Hood robbed the rich to feed the poor. Robert Kett fought the rich so the poor could feed themselves.

Chapter 12
Tracks and Trails

The most recent addition commemorating Robert Kett and his rebellion is Kett's Country Walk. The promotional blurb for the Walk says it was inspired by 'the 16th century activities of Robert Kett.' I've taken the bus from Norwich to Wymondham. It's a short, 8 mile ride. I make my way to the Abbey and ponder the fate of Robert Kett's brother, William, whose death must have been lingering and slow as he hung in chains on the walls of the tower. But today, the Abbey and its grassy grounds are peaceful and quiet. I'm here to walk part of the route named after the town's famous rebel. At first I'm not sure where the Walk begins but after a few false starts and repeated looks at the map, I eventually get to where I need to be. My plan is to spend the day strolling back to Norwich, or at least as far as time and stamina allow. The early morning drizzle has cleared and I'm walking into the lightest of easterly breezes.

The contrived walk begins in Wymondham and meanders for 21 miles towards Norwich. Surprisingly it doesn't pass anywhere near Kett's Oak. Nor does it visit Mousehold Heath where Kett made his camp beneath the Restoration Oak. The Walk's rather gentle character sees it 'taking in a number of churches', villages and country paths. The ambling, rambling state of mind of the modern-day Kett Country walker no doubt is very different to the agitated, angry and excited condition of the original rebels.

The Walk ends in Cringleford on the outskirts of Norwich but if you are minded you can carry on along the city's roads to where another of the county's splendid walks begins, the Marriott's Way. This is yet one more of the many trails, bridleways and paths that criss and cross Norfolk. The Marriott's Way takes you on a 26 mile path from Norwich to Aylsham. It takes advantage of two disused railway lines originally built by the Midland and Great Northern Joint Railway. Fittingly, the Way is named after the railway company's chief engineer, William Marriott who died in Sheringham, 1943, aged 86.

Marriott's Way and Kett's Country Walk are just two of the 1,200 miles of paths, bridleways and cycle routes that make up the Norfolk Trails network. Like the Marriott's Way, sections of other paths also follow disused railway tracks including the Paston Way as it heads off north east out of North Walsham.

When you look at an Ordnance Survey map of Norfolk, similar to many other counties, it is staggering to see how many disused and dismantled railways there are, depicted by short bursts of tapered hatched black lines. The overgrown lines, now silent, weave and wander between towns and villages across the county – King's Lynn to East Dereham, Swaffham to Thetford, Wells-next-the-Sea to Fakenham, North Walsham to Overstrand. You see their buried and ghostly remains wherever you walk. There are long straight runs of raised earth now covered in trees. You come across cuttings carved through gently undulating fields and woods. Defunct bridges straddle quiet country roads. There are houses with platforms that were once stations.

There is an easy path that takes you north across fields and hills from Southrepps to the coastal town of Overstrand. It was a spring day and I had taken the train to Gunton from where I planned to walk, via the coast, to Cromer. As I was approaching the outskirts of Overstrand and stepping down the steep, gladed slopes of the Cromer Ridge, I noticed a long straight section of land that was obviously once an old railway track. At the point where the path crossed the line, there was evidence of brick arches, a bridge and what appeared to be an old railway station now masquerading as a private house. There was a man working in the gardens. I asked him if the house was Overstrand train station.

'Yes, that's right. You're a bit late, though, boy. You just missed the last one.'

The last train had trundled out of the station in April 1953. There was another occasion when I had taken the train from Norwich to London. A few miles into the journey, there was an engine failure. We all had to get off and wait on the platform of Diss station. There was an announcement: 'There will be a replacement train in five minutes. We apologise for any inconvenience.' Five minutes later a train roared through the station at 80 mph. A Norfolk old boy gave a baleful look as the train rushed by, then turned to me and said:

'Ain't got the hang of this stoppin' business, have they.'

Overstrand station closed, then, in 1953. It was part of the North Norfolk and Suffolk Joint Railway company which had lines connecting many of the east coast towns and resorts between Lowestoft and Cromer. The first railway arrived in Norfolk in 1845. In the following years, a frenzy of railway building occurred. At one time Norwich had three railway stations (now it has only one). In 1848 Amelia Opie was thrilled to report her first ride on a train, from Norwich to London. What had taken her a couple of days by coach now took only a morning.

New lines appeared all over the county, many bringing holiday makers to the coastal towns, resorts, and the Norfolk Broads. Grand hotels and boarding houses appeared in Great Yarmouth, Mundesley, Cromer and Hunstanton.

New railway companies sprang up to build the lines – the Northern and Eastern Railway, the Norwich and Brandon Railway, Eastern Railway Union, the Midland and Great Northern Joint Railway. As time went by, the companies began to consolidate. By the 1920s, the dominant player became known as the London and North Eastern Railway (LNER), although for a while the Midland and Great Northern Joint Railway (M&GNJR) remained separate including the time when William Marriott was chief engineer and general traffic manager.

The M&GNJR had a major steam locomotive building and maintenance facility at, of all the unlikely places, Melton Constable, a village seven miles south of Blakeney. At the turn of the 20th century, the works dominated the local economy and the little town became known as 'the Crewe of North Norfolk'. But the last train chugged out of Melton Constable in 1964.

Once a hub for trains to King's Lynn, Cromer, Great Yarmouth, Fakenham and Norwich, all that can be seen in Melton Constable today are the fading scars of four dismantled railway tracks converging on the village from north, south, east and west. The sheds, the lines and the workshops have long gone and the site is now a small industrial estate.

In 1947 all British railway companies became nationalised, creating British Railways, imaginatively shortened in 1965 to British Rail, no doubt after expensive advice from 1960s' marketing men.

A national review of British Railways carried out by Dr Richard Beeching in 1962 led to the infamous Beeching Report. It recommended the closure of thousands of miles of track and hundreds of stations across the country. Norfolk didn't escape. The Beeching Axe as it became known resulted in the county losing two thirds of its railway stations and most of its branch lines. A TV sitcom reworked the Flanagan and Allen song of 'Oh! Mr Porter' capturing the public's mood of the time:

> Oh! Dr Beeching, what have you done?
> There were once lots of trains to catch, but soon there will be none.
> I'll have to buy a bike 'cause I can't afford a car
> Oh! Dr Beeching! What a naughty man you are!

Today Norfolk has a mainline intercity track running from Norwich to London. There is a slower cross country route that rattles west to Thetford and beyond. And there are a handful of branch lines to Cromer and Sheringham, Yarmouth and

Lowestoft, Downham Market and King's Lynn. And that's it. There is not even a British Rail anymore. Legislation to privatise and break up the railways was passed in 1993. At the end of the process, the country was left with 25 separate train operating companies, several freight train franchises and one company responsible for most of the track and infrastructure known as Network Rail.

Nearly three quarters of the train franchises are now owned by foreign train operators and other countries' state run rail services who, in many cases, like the Angles, Saxons and Normans before them moved in from Germany, Holland and France…and took over. As I write this, the Norwich to London trains are currently run by Abellio Greater Anglia. Abellio is the international arm of the Dutch national train operator, Nederlandse Spoorwegan with its headquarters in Utrecht.

Railways have always attracted enthusiasts, especially those in love with steam. The efforts of these dedicated men and women have left us with short runs of railway line rescued or revived from the Beeching axe. These strips of bygone railway now find themselves stranded in both time and place, lines that take you a few miles there and then a few miles back, but wonderful all the same. These are the heritage lines and Norfolk has several.

The North Norfolk Railway in one such line. It was originally built by our friend, William Marriott. The railway is also known as the Poppy Line. Its many splendid steam engines puff between Sheringham and Holt, between banks of primroses and bluebells in Spring, and fields of poppies in Summer.

A few years ago, when I was younger and could do these things, I was half way through a 100 mile long bike ride. It was a charity event organised by the Norfolk British Heart Foundation. The circuit started and finished in Norwich. The northern stretch brushed the North Norfolk coast. On my old, heavy-duty commuter bike, I was pretty clapped out by the time I had reached the 50 mile mark. All those men and women in lycra, riding their expensive carbon-fibre framed lightweight machines, had passed me some time ago. I was in amongst the slow, sure and steady fun riders.

It was as I was leaving Sheringham, cycling along the Weybourne Road, that I was jolted out of a mindless, happy fatigue by the unexpected sound of a steam train's whistle. And there, silhouetted, with clouds of white smoke and steam billowing into a cerulean sky, was a Poppy Line train pulling coaches full of holiday makers.

At this point, for a few hundred yards the track runs parallel with the road. The train steamed its way along on slightly raised ground, the sea to its north and the road a few yards below to the south. As the people on the puffing train spotted us puffing on our bikes, they waved and laughed encouragingly as they overtook us. I pedalled faster just to try and keep up. But of course I failed. A magical few moments though.

The serious cyclists, the men and women in lycra, completed the ride in just over four hours. I finished in just under eight. The less said about the ride home from the finish line in Cathedral Close the better.

I guess for everyone of my generation, the sight, sound and smell of a steam engine evokes all kinds of memories. As a 10 year old, my feral friends and I collected train numbers. It was the craze. We would tick them off, or more specifically underline them, in one of the Ian Allan books which listed every locomotive's number, type, class and region. We spotted the engines as they went about their noisy, smelly, sooty, muscular business. I lived close to a railway line. There was nothing I enjoyed more than standing on the low walled bridge with my head over the side waiting for a train to thunder below in a fury of steam and smoke, clatter and heat.

A heritage track also runs between Wymondham and Dereham. This is the Mid-Norfolk Railway, currently 14 miles long but with plans to recover and restore more of the old route. And there are smaller gauge light railways to be found along the

Bure Valley, running from Wroxham to Aylsham and between Wells and Walsingham.

There is something visceral about a steam locomotive huffing and puffing along a railway track. You can see, smell, feel even, how the engine works. Coal and heat, fire and water, steam and pistons, condensers and wheels. You grasp the mechanics. Unlike so much of today's world of onboard computers, electronic circuits and lasers which for most of us remain unfathomable as they do whatever they do beneath laptop keyboards and shiny car bonnets, these industrial age machines of fire and steam can be understood. The hundreds of volunteers and enthusiasts who restore the engines and keep the lines running seem inspired by both the science and the emotion, the engineering and excitement of this bygone age of steam and smoke. I get it.

At the end of the Poppy Line is Holt and at Holt you can visit the William Marriott Museum, also run by the M&GN Joint Railway Society. Topographical traces of the old line, once more marked as 'dismantled railway' on Ordnance Survey maps, can still be found heading out of Holt, south towards Melton Constable, west to Fakenham, before finally ending up in King's Lynn.

One of the people who originally pushed for a railway to be built between King's Lynn and Fakenham was Prebendary Joseph Brereton, rector of St. Andrew's church, Little Massingham. We first met the Reverend Brereton many pages back. It was he who, in 1873, helped found the Norfolk County School at North Elmham which later became Watts Naval College.

The vicar was generally enthusiastic about all things rail and most things educational. His father had been vicar at Little Massingham and prior to his death, Joseph had been a priest in Devon where he had helped establish the Devon County School which later became known as West Buckland School. While in North Devon, he joined others to make the case for the Devon and Somerset Railway company to build a line from Taunton to Barnstaple. The case was successful.

After his father's death, Joseph returned to his birthplace and like his father before him, became rector of St Andrew's Church at Little Masssingham. The railway line from King's Lynn to Little Massingham was opened in 1879 along with a station that served the village and surrounding settlements. A year later the line was extended to Fakenham.

Having also successfully founded the Norfolk County School for the sons of artisans and farmers at North Elmham on the banks of the River Wensum, the vicar could think of nothing more fitting to round off his achievement than to give the school its own railway station. And that's what he got.

The Norfolk County School station was situated roughly half way between Dereham and Fakenham on the original Wymondham, Dereham, Fakenham and Wells-next-the-Sea line which first opened in 1847. The Reverend Brereton was convinced that the school needed its own station and so he lobbied vigorously for one to be built. The new station opened in 1886. Even when the school was sold and became the Watts Naval School, the station kept its original name. But in 1952, the line closed to passenger traffic and with it the station.

In the late 1990s, the heritage railway group – the Mid-Norfolk Railway (MNR) Preservation Trust – bought the station, restored and repainted it. It is now a visitor centre for those who wish to walk the quiet ways around the Wensum valley and look at the remains of the Anglo-Saxon Cathedral and the Bishop's Palace half a mile south in the village of North Elmham itself. And on your return, why not have a cup of tea in the station tea room, though its opening times are rather limited.

There are also some very long term plans by the MNR enthusiasts to restore the line all the way from Dereham to Fakenham, with trains calling once more at the County School station. The Reverend Brereton, who is buried in the churchyard at Little Massingham, must be chugging with delight in his grave.

North Elmham lies pretty much at the centre of the county. Perhaps it has some strange gravitational pull on the people, places and history flung around it. It keeps cropping up in this book of wanderings. It is where lines of time repeatedly meet and cross. It refuses to fade. North Elmham was where the Anglo-Saxons built their spiritual centre in a cathedral of wood which, when it became redundant, was where the first Bishop of Norwich, Herbert de Losinga, constructed his chapel. Two hundred years later, Henry le Despencer, the nineteenth consecrated Bishop of Norwich, turned the chapel into a fortified house. And then 500 years later, another priest felt the village was the best place to build a school, the Norfolk County School, for the sons of farmers and aritisans, served by its own station.

Back in the late 19th century, it would have been possible for the Reverend Joseph Brereton to catch a train from his home village of Little Massingham to the County School station to visit the school which he founded. He would only have had to make one change at Fakenham. Whether or not, or how often he made this journey, we don't know, but given his enthusiasm for railways, I'd like to think he was a regular traveller on the complex network of lines that the Victorian engineers had built across Norfolk. But like the Dereham to Fakenham route, the King's Lynn to Fakenham line eventually ran out of steam and closed in 1959, and with it the vicar's home station at Little Massingham. The waiting rooms and ticket office buildings have been converted into private houses.

Little Massingham, though no longer in possession of a railway line, is crossed on its western edges by the Peddars Way. The Way is a long distance footpath that runs north north east in an almost straight line from just east of Thetford to the coast at Holme next the Sea. It is 46 miles long.

Many think its origins are pre-Roman. The ancient Britons, including Norfolk's Iceni people, were great traders. Whenever possible, they took the most direct route to wherever they were going. But the tracks were moderated by geography and geology, the lines of least resistance, the drier ground, the least dangerous. The simple act of feet, thousands of feet over hundreds of years, tramping over the same ground gradually created networks and trails all over England.

However, the ruler-straight line of the Peddars Way suggests a Roman influence. Even the name hints at Roman ancestory – *pedester*, Latin, on foot. Quite why there should be a Roman highway from Suffolk to Holme next the Sea is not entirely clear. If it was a military road, there might have been a the need to get troops up to the coast to defend against the ever-present threat of marauding Angles and Saxons. If it was also a trading route, it offered a direct road to the North Norfolk ports which in Roman times could take sea going ships with ease.

At its southern end, the Peddars Way connects with the Icknield Way. Some believe that it is possible to link a series of pathways, all of Neolithic origin, from Lyme Regis in Dorset, across Salisbury Plain, over the Downs of Berkshire and on to the Chilterns, up along the chalk lands of Cambridgeshire and Suffolk before joining the Peddars Way in Norfolk. Keeping to higher ground, especially the chalk hills, the route is thought to be one of oldest roads in Britain. The walker and writer, Ray Quinlan, names the whole 363 mile stretch from Dorset to Holme next the Sea *The Greater Ridgeway*.

When it reaches Holme next the Sea, the Peddars Way takes a right turn and tracks into the North Norfolk Coastal Path. For 45 miles, this dreamy trail wanders along beaches, in and out of creeks, takes in nature reserves and bird sanctuaries, and drifts through an Area of Outstanding Natural Beauty. As it ambles east, it visits the old ports and seaside villages of Brancaster, the Burnhams, Holkham, Wells-next-the-Sea, Blakeney, Cley next the Sea, Sheringham, East and West Runton, past the exhumed grave of the 700,000 year old mammoth, and finally on to Cromer.

Beyond Cromer, the North Norfolk Coastal Path turns south and morphs into another long distance trail – the 61 mile long Weaver's Way. Like many modern trails, it has been concocted out of many smaller paths, old bridleways, and disused railway lines. It is named in honour of East Norfolk's wool rich past and weaving history. The Way begins in Cromer and weaves (sorry) its way inland, south via North Walsham, to Great Yarmouth, passing by, properly enough, the village of Worstead.

On its journey south, The Weaver's Way takes a sinuous route around several of Norfolk's Broads. Here, amongst these hidden rivers and lakes, we are reminded again that land and sea, seemingly a constant, timeless presence, are mere passing arrangements of the elements, transient. They shift and change, come and go.

We remember that 10,000 years ago as the temperatures rose and the great ice sheets melted, sea levels slowly rose. The rivers of East Anglia that once flowed out onto the plains of Doggerland began to make their way into the rising North Sea. As the waters rose, their seaward journeys became shorter. Their flow slowed as gradients fell. The hills wore lower, the seas washed higher, and so the rivers simply had less of a drop before they reached the open waters.

As a result, the rivers and streams became sluggish. The low land around turned swampy, weed-rich, reed-rich, fen-like. Each year the dead and dying vegetation sank and accumulated on the bottom of the marshy flood plains, compacting under the weight of more and more decaying matter. The result was peat, layers and layers of peat – in this case, the Middle Peat of Norfolk that first began to accumulate around 5,000 years ago. The Middle Peat is the thickest of the peat layers and can be up to sixteen feet deep in parts.

It was toward the end of this Middle Peat period, about 2,200 years ago, that another major rise in sea level occurred. The sea crept inland through coastal breaks at Winterton and Sea Palling, Horsey and Waxham, and along the River Yare at Yarmouth itself. The rivers of East Norfolk – the Bure, Thurne and Ant – became first inland marine mudflats, and then saltmarshes, bogs and fens rich in plants and reed beds. But in time they too began to silt up, sinking to form thin beds of clay, silt and finally more peat – the Upper Peat Bed.

By the 1st century AD, the British tribes had succumbed to Roman occupation. By the 4th and 5th centuries, the Roman Empire itself was in decline. This gave the tribes from North Germany and Denmark the chance to invade, settle and farm. Anglo-Saxon Norfolk gradually developed into a busy and productive place. Forests were cleared to free the land for ploughing. Oak and elm were felled for timber to build houses. Wood was cut and gathered for fuel, and acre by acre, the woodlands shrank. There was less fuel to keep the fires burning and the forges hot. And so the enterprising Saxons and later, the labouring peasants of feudal Norfolk began to look down as well as up for their fuel. They learned to dig peat as well as fell wood.

As the cutters dug deeper and deeper, the sides of the peat excavations became steep, sheer and stepped. Over hundreds of years, vast amounts of peat were cut, dried and burned. The fuel was sent to the cities and towns, the abbeys and hamlets, Norwich and the Cathedral.

As more and more peat was exploited, large hollows, often separated by narrow strips, began to pit the low, open valleys. However, the medieval climate was getting gradually wetter. The rains were heavier. Sea levels again rose. It was getting more difficult to cut the peat. Flooding was an ever-present danger. And finally, with the import of coal, the cost and effort of recovering the peat became just too much.

When the diggings were finally abandoned in the 14th and 15th centuries, the rivers seeped and soaked their way in, quietly taking back what had always been theirs. Lakes formed in the scoops and hollows. These became known as broads. Narrow cuts and dykes link one broad with another. And flowing slowly between, through and by the broads are the Rivers – the Bure, Thurne, Ant, Chet, Wensum, Yare, and to the south, Waveney.

The Broads, as the area is known today, sunk into a watery world. The rivers, lakes and dykes became bordered by beds of reed, swampy woodland and flat expanses of marsh and field. The wetlands began to attract an astonishing variety of wildlife, especially birds – bitterns, mallards and geese; grebes, coots and herons; cormorants, kestrels and sparrowhawks. And over time, the Broads became the home of the marshmen, the Broadlanders who fished, hunted and cut the reeds for thatch.

As birds of all descriptions were attracted to the Broads, so too was the pioneering bird photographer, Miss Emma Turner. She was born in Kent in 1866. In 1900 she decided to take up photography. In the same year, she also met the naturalist and bird photographer Richard Kearton. It was one of his lectures that inspired Emma to photograph birds herself.

In 1902, she found her way to Norfolk and the Broads where she settled for the next twenty five years. Soon after her arrival, she befriended two local marshmen – Alfred Nudd and keeper Jim Vincent. Her ambition was to photograph all the birds of Broadland.

Her base was Hickling Broad, the largest of the Broads, stretching a mile or two long and up to a mile wide. (See *Plate 17*) Emma found a swampy island off the edge of the marsh on which she built a small hut. It had a thatched roof, a wood burner, and equipment to develop some of her photographic plates. Local marshmen still refer to the place as Turner Island although the hut has long since disappeared.

As well as a sailing boat and canoe, she also had a houseboat built for herself, moored on Hickling Broad. The boat was fashioned to her own design and was launched on 18 March 1905. She named the boat *Water Rail* after the first marsh bird she photographed. And that's where she lived, with her dogs, for most of the next twenty years, viewed as an eccentric by the locals but also regarded with affection.

Although unconventional, Emma Turner was by no means a loner. Amongst her friends was the East Anglian naturalist, diarist and writer, the splendidly and appropriately named Reverend Maurice Charles Hinton Bird, rector of Brunstead, a hamlet a few miles north of Hickling Broad. His knowledge of Norfolk bird life was said to be second to none. However, it was Emma who wrote and illustrated the first major book on the subject, *Broadland Birds*, published in 1924, a year before the Reverend died.

Emma first achieved fame in 1911. With the help of Jim Vincent, she took a photograph of a young bittern. Up until then it was thought that bitterns had stopped breeding in Britain. The last sighting of a nesting bittern had been in 1886. But the presence of the young bird in the reed beds of Hickling Broad suggested otherwise. Emma and Jim's sighting coupled with the photographic evidence to back it was a cause of great celebration amongst ornithologists.

Since Emma's day, the bittern has gradually re-established itself as a breeding bird in Britain. On a still spring morning, you can hear the male bittern's low, haunting boom and if you are very lucky, you might just catch a glimpse of its low, slow, leisurely flight over the grey brown waters of a broad..

To get as close as she could to her subjects, Emma would often cover herself in the marshy vegetation and lie still in the muddy reeds with her large, heavy plate-camera, waiting for water rail, redshanks, warblers, snipe, cranes, teals, and marsh harriers to come into view. Once a glass plate had been exposed, the camera had to be re-loaded with a fresh one. Time and patience as well as knowledge and skill were needed to get even one picture. Emma didn't limit herself to the Broads. For a short time, she was the first resident warden for the National Trust on Scolt Head, North Norfolk, internationally important for its populations of terns. By this time, she had equipped herself with one of the new single lens reflex cameras. Her time as warden led to the publication of another book, *Bird Watching on Scolt Head*.

Towards the end of her life, Emma moved to Cambridge where she became vice-president of the Cambridge Bird Club. She was awarded a Gold Medal by the Royal Photographic Society and was one of the first women to be admitted as a Fellow of the Linnaean Society, London, one of whose founding members and first President was Sir James Smith, the botanist, born in Norwich, December 1759, the son of a wealthy wool merchant.

If Emma was a pioneer of photographing, popularising and writing about British birds, then Sir James was equally successful in writing about and promoting interest in British plants. His books were beautifully illustrated by James Sowerby. *Flora Britannica* and *The English Flora* are still held in high regard. After his marriage, Sir James moved back to Norwich in 1797. He died in 1824. He has a memorial dedicated to him on the walls of St Peter Mancroft Church just a few yards below the chancel where Sir Thomas Browne has his final resting place. Smith the botanist and Browne the physician had much in common and it seems fitting that memorials to their lives should find themselves within chatting distance beneath the roof of the church of St Peter Mancroft.

Emma Turner's success was sealed when she was elected an Honorary member of the British Ornithologists' Union, generally regarded at the time as a male preserve. She died on 13 August 1940, aged 74 years. Her prose style was as lyrical as her photographs were beautiful. Here, in a quote from her book, *Broadland Birds*, she gently seduces the reader into the quiet, watery beauty of the Broads:

> Just what it is in the marshlands that grips the imagination and casts a spell over its lovers I do not know. We none of us know. It is a land of wide, windswept spaces and far flung horizons, of mystic nights and great silences. In the daytime it is a shifting kaleidoscope of colour. Every hour of the day and every day in the year brings its own quota of light, colour and sound… Each mood has its charms and is capable of infinite variations.

The Weavers Way loops around and between many of the broads, including Hickling Broad. It is mid-week and I've decided to treat myself to walk along the middle sections of the Way. The dead flat track loops and twists. More often than not, I have no sense of the rivers and open waters that can sometimes be only a few yards away. The flatness of the landscape, the dense wet woodlands, and the tall reed beds keep the Broads hidden, seen only by those who take to the waters. What I do see, though, as I wander the Way are the sails of the boats as they tack along unseen rivers. Triangles of sail-white glide silently across fields against the ruler-straight line of the distant horizon.

The Weavers Way carries on south, by Hickling Broad, crosses the Bure, reaches Acle, then loops south and east to Halvergate and the marshes of the Yare. Here the land is wide, open and flat. It is fretted with hundreds of small dykes and drainage cuttings. There are no trees. The only breaks on the skyline are the old windmills that once pumped water in the never ending task of keeping the land drained. These are the landscapes, endless and flat, that Pierre Drieu la Rochelle said induce 'horizontal vertigo'.

The road and railway tracks from Norwich to Yarmouth run for long stretches across these flatlands in dead straight lines. It's when the Weavers Way crosses the train track that you see the Berney Arms Mill and the recently closed Berney Arms pub. They sit on the northern bank of the River Yare less than half a mile before it joins the River Waveney. The sun is shining today. The sky is a thin, milky blue as I gaze east and see the hazy grey outlines of Great Yarmouth, its houses, churches, bridges and port.

The path I am on follows the river seaward as it opens out into the shimmering shallows of Breydon water before narrowing once more to form the deep water port and quayside of Great Yarmouth itself. As the Weavers Way once more crosses the River Bure, and as it is about to flow into the Yare, the path immediately changes name and becomes the westward heading Angles Way, Yarmouth to Thetford, 93 miles long, the fourth and final of Norfolk's long distance paths.

For the first few miles, the Angles Way returns along the River Yare but on the opposite, southern bank to the Weavers Way. It then meets the Waveney and it is this river's valley that guides the major part of the walk, first by the outskirts of Lowestoft and then inland where it spills over onto the very northern edges of Suffolk, through Bungay, then back into Norfolk, by Diss towards Redgrave and the source of the River Waveney itself.

The River Waveney rises less than a mile north of the village of Redgrave. As unlikely as it seems in this low lying, fen-type, peat-cut, plant rich landscape, a mere 84 feet above sea level, this is where we find the watershed between two of the region's major river systems – the Waveney and the Little Ouse. Between the two headwaters, only a few yards apart, runs the north-south B1113 South Lopham (Norfolk) to Redgrave (Suffolk) road. (See *Plate 18*)

Here, the source waters of the River Waveney collect, pond and flow east to Yarmouth. A few yards across the road in another wettish, pool-dappled, wooded patch is the source of the Little Ouse River. Admittedly, the source of the Little Ouse is not obvious, but it is here in the boggy ground that it begins its journey. It flows in the opposite direction to the Waveney, coursing west to Thetford, gradually growing in size from a damp wood, to a trickle, to a brook, to a stream, to a river.

At Thetford, the Little Ouse is joined by the River Thet. It continues north and west, through Brandon and out onto the Fens where it eventually connects with the River Great Ouse, south of Downham Market. The River Great Ouse heads north, draining the Fens before finally reaching King's Lynn and the Wash.

When you look at a map of the county, it's not too fanciful to suggest that the two rivers act moat-like, offering a watery boundary to the south and west. This fancy leaves Norfolk as an island with rivers running from Yarmouth to Thetford, Thetford to Downham Market, and Downham Market to King's Lynn. To the north and east are the Wash and the North Sea. Island Norfolk. There is, incidently, another Norfolk Island that lies in the south west corner of the Pacific Ocean, a few hundred miles north west of New Zealand and about a thousand miles east of Australia. The small island – much smaller than county Norfolk – is one of Australia's external territories. It has a population of about 2,000 and was originally named in 1774 by Captain James Cook after Mary Howard, the Duchess of Norfolk.

I am not sure at what point the upper reaches of the Waveney and Little Ouse rivers become navigable by kayak, but the idea of a watery rim poses the possibility of boating almost around the whole county, save for a few miles of soggy woods, small brooks and shallow rivers somewhere between Diss and Thetford. If the kayak was light enough, I guess it could be carried this short distance. And if the kayak was sturdy enough, it could cope with a paddle around the Wash, along the coastal waters of the North Sea and back to Yarmouth and the mouth of the River Yare. Now there's a challenge.

The geographical oddity of these two major rivers arising just a few feet apart, flowing in opposite directions, separated only by the tarmac of a small minor road less than a hundred feet above sea level had long fascinated me. So one early Spring morning I decide to take a look.

I've arrived and I'm looking north standing in the middle of the B1113 between the soggy, wooded headwaters of the Waveney on one side and the Little Ouse River on the other. And then a curious thought strikes me. The day is wet. It dawns on me that the rain falling on my right is draining into the damp woods around the source of the Waveney. Each one of these rain drops is destined to flow east until it eventually find its way to Great Yarmouth and out into the North Sea. The rain drizzling on my left is trickling into the ponds and marshy ground that marks the vague beginnings of the Little Ouse River. From here, each drop will puddle and pool with the millions of other drops and from there they will flow and meander west, then north before finding their way to King's Lynn and out into the Wash, 90 miles further up and around the coast from Great Yarmouth.

No mountain heights or knife-sharp divides here, and yet the subtlest of dips, the slightest of slopes, imperceptible to the eye, determine the life course of each drop of spring rain or flake of winter snow as it falls on to the cambered tarmac of the B1113 half way between Redgrave and South Lopham. Chance events. A gentle breeze, the spray of a passing car, the rippled surface of the road, and the watery story goes this way or that, east or west, Yarmouth or Kings Lynn. A fast approaching car snaps me out of my reverie and I make a quick dash to the Waveney side of the road. The driver stares at me with a puzzled look.

The Angles Way continues to track along the southern edges of the Waveney, through Redgrave Fen, across the divisive B1113, and then ambles west, roughly following the Little Ouse. Just before it reaches the eastern fringes of Thetford, the Angles Way makes a right-angled approach to the north-south running Peddars Way at the point where the Icknield Way joins it from

Suffolk. We are back where we started. The walk has taken us in a great circle around the county's perimeter, clockwise from Thetford via Holme next the Sea, Holkham Beach, Blackeney, Cromer, the Broads, Great Yarmouth, the outskirts of Lowestoft, Beccles, Bungay, Diss, the valley of the Little Ouse River and back to Thetford.

The Peddars Way, the North Norfolk Coastal Path, the Weavers Way and the Angles Way form a huge 245 mile loop around the fringes of Norfolk. The trails follow roman roads and Victorian railways, rivers and fen, broads and brecks, creeks and sea. Over the years I have walked many sections of these ways but I have never completed the loop as one, whole challenge. My approach has been piecemeal. It would be tempting, though, to wander the ways over a couple of weeks, lunching in pubs and plotting where to stop and have overnight bed and breakfast. Another day. Perhaps.

Chapter 13
Love and Life

George Borrow, if he had been alive today, would claim, no doubt, to need only three days to walk the 245 mile Norfolk circuit. Will Kemp might have taken a happy month of fine weather to dance his way around the ring. And quite a few pages back, we briefly met two writer-walkers as they were about to set off south along the Icknield Way. They were on the outskirts of Thetford, at the point where the Peddars Way ends its southerly trek and rambles into the Icknield Way. But the two men didn't set off together. Nearly a hundred years separated their walks, but there is a link.

In his book of paths, tracks and ancient ways – *The Old Ways* – Robert Macfarlane is inspired by the words and wanderings of the poet and writer Edward Thomas. He decides to follow in the poet's footsteps:

> ...on a late-May morning I left from my Cambridge home to walk what is often claimed to be the most ancient land route in Britain, the Icknield Way, which Edward Thomas had walked and bicycled a century earlier. It was the first of my foot-journeys.

Thomas had begun his walk in 1913, a year before the Great War in which he would die.

Whether it's walkers who write or writers who walk, in all cases the act of putting one foot in front of the other and falling into that metronomical rhythm can cast the individual into philosophical mood. Often the mood conjured can be joyous, up-beat, even ecstatic. George Borrow could certainly walk himself out of his depressions – his 'horrors'.

Lavengro is one of Borrow's remarkable books, first published in 1851. It is part memoir, part autobiography, part novel. On his extraordinary travels, Borrow meets the gypsy, Jasper Petulengro. They talk about life and death. Jasper is glad to be alive, out in the open, on the road. He feels the wind, the summer's warmth, the rain. He sees the sun, moon and stars. For him, life is sweet and he is glad to be alive:

> There's night and day, brother, both sweet things; sun, moon, and stars, brother, all sweet things: there's likewise a wind on the heath. Life is very sweet, brother; who would wish to die? ... There's the wind on the heath, brother, if only I could feel that, I would gladly live for ever…

Richard Holmes also walks. He is a biographer, a one-time lecturer at the University of East Anglia, partner of the novelist Rose Tremain, and Norfolk resident. Richard knows how mountains and sky, wind and rain can take you out of yourself and then carry you back with senses tingling. Already determined to become a biographer, as a young man he set out to retrace the journeys made by various Romantic figures. He describes his travels and the people he follows in his wonderful book *Footsteps: Adventures of a Romantic Biographer*.

Holmes visited Paris and reflected on the life of Mary Wollstonecroft, political philosopher, pioneering champion of women's rights, and inspiration for Amelia Opie. Mary moved to the city in 1792, the time of the French Revolution. One of the people Mary met during her stay in Paris was the Thetford radical, Thomas Paine. Only a year after the appearance of Paine's first volume of *Rights of Man*, Mary published *A Vindication of the Rights of Women* in 1792.

Holmes also goes to Italy. There, he explores the lives of the poet Percy Bysshe Shelley and his young wife, Mary Shelley, the novelist and, as it happens, the daughter of Mary

Wollstonecroft. As we learned earlier, Mary Wollstonecroft died a few days after her daughter's birth and the baby was raised by her father, the political philosopher, William Godwin In her late teens, the young Mary, née Godwin, began an affair with the poet, Percy Bysshe Shelley. He was already married. It was only after Shelley's wife Harriett committed suicide that the couple finally wed in 1816. Two years later, the now Mrs Mary Shelley wrote and published her novel, *Frankenstein.*

But it is when Holmes is retracing Robert Louis Stevenson's travels in France that we become struck by both men's stamina and the musings that their walks inspire. In 1878 Robert Louis Stevenson spent several weeks in France walking in the Cevénnes. He was accompanied on his journey by Modestine, a donkey 'the size of a large Newfoundland dog and the colour of "an ideal mouse"' who carried his baggage and offered him company. Stevenson wrote a book based on his walk, *Travels with a Donkey in the Cevénnes*. He explains:

> For my part, I travel not to go anywhere, but to go; I travel for travel's sake... the great affair is to move; to feel the needs and hitches of life a little more nearly; to get down off this featherbed of civilisation, and to find the globe granite underfoot and strewn with cutting flints.

In 1964, Holmes followed in the Scotsman's footsteps, *sans* donkey. He wanted to see and feel and think the journey as Stevenson might have done. And so Holmes learned to write a distinctive and evocative style of biography.

Stevenson would sometimes sleep out in the open air. The young Holmes does the same, sleeping rough under the stars. The wide outdoors, breathing in the clear, fresh air, takes the men outside of themselves into the landscape and then back again, bringing about a heightened sense of being. During one ecstatic moment Stevenson swears he will never sleep in a bed again:

In the whole of my life I have never tasted a more perfect hour of life…O sancta Solitudo! I was such a world away from the roaring streets, the delivery of cruel letters, and the saloons where people love to talk, that it seemed to me that life had begun afresh, and I knew no one in all the universe but the almighty maker. I promised myself, as Jacob set up an altar, that I should never again sleep under a roof if I could help it, so gentle, so cool, so singularly peaceful and large were my sensations.

Holmes follows suit as he contemplated the beauty all about. For him, it felt like 'grasping for breath in a rolling blue sea of hills going southwards as far as the sky and further – being washed entirely away by it all – exalted and lonely as hell'. He continues:

I lay for hours on my back in the heather watching the clouds troop endlessly and majestically overhead in the blue. If you were dead and buried, I thought, that is how life would go on around you; that is how Stevenson would see it. And of course I recited his epitaph, known by heart, to generations of English children like me:

> Here he lies where he longed to be;
> Home is the sailor, home from the sea,
> And the hunter home from the hill.

But walking in big landscapes or through wild weather can also excite other feelings, ones of smallness and insignificance which, in their own overwhelming way, can equally thrill. I had these sensations on Holkham Beach where sand, sea and sky merge and become one. It is nature's infinite, eternal, sublime beauty and utter indifference that puts our short, tiny lives into perspective even as our senses dissolve elementally, transcendentally into the heart stopping boundlessness and timelessness into which we can be momentarily cast. We live for a bright, brief moment in a crack of light, say the poets, between two eternities of darkness, between two endless nights. But how glorious that light can be, how breathtaking those moments when you are high on a mountain top or alone beneath the big skies of a North Norfolk beach.

For some, the bright moments intensify, become more immediate as we reach our own end. This was beautifully described by Dennis Potter, the television dramatist, three months before his own death on 7 June 1994. He knew he was soon to die of pancreatic cancer. In March of that year, Potter agreed to be interviewed by Melvyn Bragg for a Channel 4 Art's programme and these were his thoughts about life and the world about him:

> Below my window…when I'm working, is a plum tree. It looks like apple blossom, you know, but it's white and looking at it, instead of saying, that's a nice blossom…now, last week, looking at it through the window when I'm writing, it is the whitest, frothiest, blossomist blossom that there ever could be. Things are both more trivial than they ever were and more important than they ever were, and the difference between the trivial and the important doesn't seem to matter, but the nowness of everything is absolutely wondrous.

It is when our senses become lost in the sights, sounds, and smells, in the keen air around and the solid earth beneath, in the rustling trees and the song of birds, in the babble of water and the scent of flowers, that we feel most alive, vibrant, bright. Our senses are heightened so exquisitely that for a few fleeting seconds we feel, literally, sensational. We simply feel. Entering the flow of experience takes us outside our bounded sense of self and time's arrow.

There is, then, a philosophy of walking, a wisdom in wandering. And many philosophers have been walkers – Kant, Hobbes, Montaigne, Rousseau, Nietzsche, Wittgenstein, Schopenhauer. The modern French philosopher, Frédéric Gros, has written a book with the title *A Philosophy of Walking*. 'You are doing nothing when you walk', he writes, 'nothing but walking. But having nothing to do but walk makes it possible to recover the pure sensation of being, to rediscover the simple joy of being…'

But there is also walking that transports the traveller inwards. Travelling out - across land, along coasts and over hills – walking can also be a journey into the self. All of this is beautifully said by that most consummate and earth-bound of nature writers, Nan Shepherd. In her book, *The Living Mountain*, she searches for the 'essential nature' of the Scottish Cairngorms and the wild world around her. For her, walking is 'a journey into Being; for as I penetrate more deeply into the mountain's life, I penetrate also into my own. For an hour I am beyond desire…I am not out of myself, but in myself: I am. To know Being; this is the final grace accorded from the mountain.' These are the book's final words. Walking takes you outside, inside, and beyond your self.

In his funny and thoughtful book, *The Lost Art of Walking*, Geoffrey Nicholson says he walks because he has to: 'I walk because it keeps me sane.' He is, though, pretty dismissive of those who get rather precious about their 'walks in nature'. He sees them trying to assert some moral and spiritual superiority over those who don't walk or those who just walk, for walking's sake. Beware, says Nicholson, of that specious trinity – walking, nature and spirituality.

However, having said that, like most walkers, he does have his moments. Walking anywhere did it for Borrow and still does it for Gros. Mountains did it for Shepherd and do it for

Macfarlane. Central France did it for Stevenson and Holmes. Norfolk's endless beaches and big skies do it for me. For Nicholson it is walking in the deserts of North America. And so he confesses, perhaps a little reluctantly, even shyly that:

> ...although by and large I don't understand spiritual and religious longings, much less spiritual and religious certainties, sometimes when I'm walking in the desert, there are moments, just moments, when I have some vague sense of over-arching well-being, something that might conceivably be what serious religious believers mean when they talk about revelation and transcendence.

So whether for pleasure or therapy, purpose or escape, sensation or solitude, walking can inspire reflection and awareness. When we walk we feel alive but if the light, the elements and scale are right, we can also have a thrilling, liberating sense of our own insignificance. And wandering in Norfolk is one of the places for conjuring such feelings and thoughts.

As a physician, Thomas Browne, the good doctor of Norwich, certainly knew about death and that much of life's meaning is to be found in living life to the full. He also knew a great deal about his adopted county of Norfolk. But quite how much walking he did along its highways and byways we don't really know. What he did know, though, was the richness of the county's natural history and archaeology. His knowledge and collecting passion helped create his own cabinet of curiosities. And like the walkers who philosophise and the philosophers who walk, his ceaseless curiosity also allowed him to write and meditate on many things, including matters of life and death, most famously in his essay *Urn Burial*, published in 1658.

In the 1650s, a large number of burial urns, made of clay, were discovered and examined by Browne in a field near Walsingham in Norfolk. They were buried in sandy soil less than three feet deep. Browne thought they were Roman cremation urns although more recent research dates them as Anglo-Saxon. In his book, *Urn Burial*, this is how Browne introduces his reflections on death and man's vain hopes on immortality.

> In a field of old Walsingham, not many months past, were digged up between fourty and fifty Urnes, deposited in dry and sandy soile, not a yard deep, not far from one another.... Some containing two pounds of bones, distinguishable in skulls, ribs, jawes, thighbones, and teeth, with fresh impressions of their combustion. Besides the extraneous substances, like peeces of small boxes, or combs, handsomely wrought, handles of small brasse instruments, brazen nippers, and in one some kinde of Opale.

The meditations inspired by the burial urns are not only wonderfully written, but at times they can also be quite funny. 'The long habit of living indisposeth us for dying...' says Browne and 'There is no antidote against the opium of time...' But in the end, we are all forgotten, sooner or later, whether rich or poor, of high rank or low. Death 'deals with the memory of men without distinction to merit perpetuity...'. Browne's contemplations on death and oblivion make him aware of life's all too short an arc. We live on the brink of nothingness. 'The night of time far surpasseth the day,' he writes, and although we might enjoy the fleeting sun, 'it cannot be long before we lie down in darkness, and have our light in ashes...' Life and our awareness of it is but a brief flicker, bracketed between two spans of endless nothingness.

However, in spite of these sombre reflections, Browne is keen to recognise that to be in life's fleeting glare is utterly worthwhile and wonderful. 'Life,' he concludes 'is a pure flame, and we live by an invisible sun within us.' Browne's Christian faith ultimately makes him an optimist. And to clinch his optimism, his own life was one of energy and zeal, endless curiosity and constant collecting of everything and anything that might be of interest.

A more focussed collector, but one equally possessed was Norfolk-born Margaret Fountaine. (See *Plate 19*) Like Browne, and echoing Jasper Lavengro, she had a passion for nature and life. In her journal she wrote:

> Freedom is the crowning joy of my life…I want to see all I can of this beautiful world before I leave it…and life is so distressingly short.

I mention Margaret for a number of reasons. Firstly because in her later childhood she lived at Eaton Grange, a large house that still stands and is only a couple of hundred yards down the road from where I am writing this today, at home. I can just about see it through the trees from my bedroom window. Eaton Grange, or Number 40 Upton Road, or even sometimes 378 Unthank Road depending on which gateway you use, is now owned by the Norfolk Community Health and Care NHS Trust.

These days the house is the home and offices of the Trust's Child Development Unit. In the top left hand corner of the Trust's web page is their logo. It appears as an orange coloured butterfly made up of tiny images of toys, people, windmills, beds, teddy bears, a stethoscope, and much else of a child-centred nature. And on the glass doors that give entry to Eaton Grange are the enlarged images of these two orange butterflies. I have no idea if this is a deliberate reference to Margaret Fountaine and the time when she lived in the old brick house.

The butterfly image is actually used across all of the Trust's activities and isn't particular to the Child Development Unit.

But for the butterflies to be on the front doors of Eaton Grange is delightfully apt. And it provides the second reason for introducing Margaret Fountaine. She was a butterfly collector. Not just any old butterfly collector, but one of extraordinary dedication, range, courage and talent.

Margaret was born on 16 May 1862, the daughter of Mary Isabella and the not-very-busy, sports-loving, pleasure-seeking Reverend John Fountaine, vicar of South Acre. Margaret's mother, Mary, was also the daughter of a priest, the Reverend Lee-Warner of Walsingham Abbey.

South Acre is a small hamlet lying a few miles north of Swaffham. It lies along the Peddars Way six miles south of Little Massingham where, during Margaret's young childhood, the Reverend Brereton was busy planning his County School and its railway station at North Elmham while just down the Way, his fellow cleric, the fun-loving Reverend Fountaine was enjoying his sport and leisure.

Margaret was the second of eight children and the eldest daughter. But when she was fifteen, her father died and the family moved to Eaton Grange, then on the south western fringes of Norwich.

Her mother seems to have been controlling and bossy. In her diary, Margaret describes her childhood as 'one meaningless punishment after another' and notes 'the boredom of life with Mamma.' She couldn't wait to get away.

There was a streak of the romantic and adventurer in Margaret. In England she felt the climate was too cold, and the men even colder. She wanted warmth and passion. Aged twenty one, she fell in love with the smooth-looking, moustachioed Septimus Hewson, an Irish chorister at Norwich Cathedral. But Septimus had a drink problem and was dismissed from the Cathedral. Nor did he seem too enthusiastic in reciprocating Margaret's affections. Feeling ill-used and let down, she busied herself with travel and visiting friends and family. It was during this time of trying to get over her unrequited love that she stayed a few days with Henry Lewes, a botanist and entomologist. It was this visit that changed the direction her life. She became a butterfly collector.

The combination of a love-life that was thwarted, a home-life that was stifling, and a climate that was cold made Margaret restless. And so when she was in her early twenties, and in possession of a decent inheritance from her paternal uncle, Edward, she began to travel abroad. It was then she started to collect butterflies in earnest. She would catch a female specimen, collect the eggs, and rear the hatched caterpillars. In this way she would end up with many butterflies from just the one catch. She would keep a few of the emergent insects for her own collection and release the rest. Her obsession, skill and patience gradually established her as an expert on the life-cycle of tropical butterflies.

Throughout her lifetime, she amassed a collection of around 23,000 specimens from every continent, all beautifully mounted in cabinet display drawers. The number of butterflies pinned to death was certainly large but she more than made up for their sacrifice by releasing a further quarter of a million of her home-reared insects back into the wild.

In 1901 she met Khalil Neimy. He became her staunch help-mate and companion. Khalil was a Greek Orthodox Syrian, educated by missionaries, and fifteen years Margaret's junior. In him, Margaret found a friend, even the possibility of a lover. She felt 'a deep devotion and true affection' for her fellow collector. He wanted to marry her, and for while they were engaged. But unbeknownst to Margaret, Khalil had a wife back home in Damascus of whom Margaret was to learn only later.

'Certainly,' she writes, 'the most interesting part of my life was spent with him. The dear companion – the constant and untiring friend and assistant in our Entomological work, travelling as we did together over all the loveliest, the wildest and often the loneliest places of this most beautiful Earth…' Khalil Neimy died of a fever in 1928.

Margaret died a decade or so later in 1940, aged 78. She died, as I guess she would have wished, while out collecting butterflies. She was on the slopes of Mount St. Benedict in Trinidad when she suffered a heart attack. Her butterfly net lay on the ground beside her.

She bequeathed her vast beautiful, colourful collection of butterflies to the Castle Museum, Norwich, where it rests today, a rainbow necropolis of the bright and short-lived. The ten splendid mahogany display cases are known as the Fountaine-Neimy collection. They could almost have been the inspiration for the final two lines of Philip Larkin's poem, *Autumn*:

> And the case of butterflies so rich it looks
> As if summer settled there and died.

Margaret also left something else to the Museum – a sealed, black lacquered box with the stipulation that it should not be opened until 15 April 1978, exactly a hundred years after she first began writing her journals as a girl of sixteen, the day the bereaved family moved to their new home at Eaton Grange in Norwich.

And so honouring her wishes, the large box was left sealed before eventually being opened two days later than the stipulated day which happened to fall on a Saturday. In the trunk were twelve ledger-sized diaries, with an accompanying note:

> Before presenting this – the Story of my Life – to those, whoever they may be, one hundred years from the date on which it was first commenced to be written, i.e. April 15: 1878, I feel it incumbent upon me to offer some sort of apology for much of what is recorded therein, especially during the first few years, when…I naturally passed through a rather profitless and foolish period of my life, such as was and no doubt still is, prevalent amongst very young girls, though perhaps

more often so then – a hundred years ago, when the education of women was also shamelessly neglected, leaving the uninitiated female to commence life with all the yearnings of nature quite unexplained to her... The greatest passion of my life...was no doubt for Septimus Hewson, and the blow I received from his heartless conduct left a scar upon my heart, which no length of time ever quite effaced.

The diaries, running to over a million words, offer a remarkably revealing account of an exceptional woman. She was brave, enthusiastic, passionate, fearless, methodical, clever, occasionally sad, rueful, and at times witty and funny, especially when she is describing her relationships with men with all their presumptions and pomposity.

Here is Margaret in a foreign hotel at the end of the 19th century having just met a young man, a Mr Brown, a fellow butterfly collector. His presence and conversation cause her to suppose:

> ...that Englishmen do make love sometimes, too, though I can't imagine what it would be like. I don't understand the material they are made of, and I never did get any distance with one, and I never shall. Not but I found Mr Brown a most delightful companion.

And at another time, back in England, she spent a musical evening in mixed company which included Mr Lockie, a man 'with a fine bass voice.' They sang duets together.

> I became aware that he was growing to love me. Why did it all end? Yet I am already almost glad, because I feel the restless love of travel and excitement, and would wonder how I could have contemplated ending my days in a little villa in West Kensington. The love of a true, good man is forever denied me... I will just

have to get all the pleasure I can from the *bad* men that I meet, that is to say going to the very edge of the precipice, but without falling over it!

One bad man she tells of meeting during her stay in Sicily is an Italian Baron. In his flirtations with Margaret, now in her mid-thirties, he makes a strenuous case for the liberating effects of free love as opposed to marriage. He says that those bound in wedlock soon become weary of each other and awaken each morning 'to find themselves forever bound together, to shiver for a life-time over the dead embers of an extinct passion.'

These were the Baron's views of life, and he taught me to feel the same, to feel that free love was the best, and often the purest – only, *not* with him!'

But although Margaret has a wonderfully complicated, sometimes comical life of love and adventure among the butterflies and across the continents, above all she remains one of the foremost entomologists and collectors of her day. She ends the covering note that goes with her diaries saying 'I leave this record of the wild and fearless life of one of the "South Acre Children", who never grew up – and who enjoyed greatly and suffered much.'

Chapter 14
The Brief and The Beautiful

Margaret Fountaine embodies the spirit of many of Norfolk's more extraordinary men and women. What unites them is their shared ability to set about life with vigour, often in spite of personal hurts and setbacks. They all learned to live life to the full, giving it content, but more than anything else, value and meaning.

Margaret was badly treated by Septimus, an Irishman with a Roman name. Queen Boudica was mightily wronged by the Romans, but turned her rage and sense of injustice to rally her Celtic tribesmen and women to do battle against the invaders. Tom Paine was an outspoken critic of inequality and injustice. He was against unwarranted privilege wherever and whenever he met it. His contemporary, Amelia Opie, wrote novels exploring the inequalities suffered by women in Georgian England. She knew the radical and feminist Mary Wollstonecroft. Margaret Fountaine was born only nine years after Amelia's death and she, too, was cross, often outraged by the inequalities suffered by women. Her whole life is a fierce determination to be her own person, to be independent, to follow her passions.

Margaret was also a contemporary of Edith Cavell. Cavell was born in 1865 in the village of Swardeston near Norwich. Margaret was already three years old. Both women were daughters of Church of England vicars. Both women fell in love with, and were spurned by weak men – Margaret with the heavy drinking Septimus, and Edith with her second cousin Eddie who tells her he can't marry because he has a 'nervous condition.' But both women learned to be intensely independent and went on to show tremendous courage.

Edith Cavell left home and for a number of years was a governess, first in Essex, then for the Gurney children at Keswick New Hall near Norwich, before finally joining a Belgium family in Brussels in 1890. In 1895, Edith returned to Swardeston to look after her sick father. It was this experience that inspired her to become a nurse. By then she was in her early thirties. She moved to London, completed her training, and quickly established herself as a skilful nurse and able manager.

In 1907 Edith found herself back in Brussels invited by Dr Antoine Depage to be matron and run the newly established L'École Belge d'Infirmières Diplômées. Her training programmes for nurses proved a great success.

In June 1914, Edith visited her widowed mother in Norfolk. As hostilities began to break out in Europe Edith decided to return to Brussels. On 4 August Germany invaded Belgium. Belgium's ally, Britain, declared war on Germany. By 20 August, the German army was in occupation of Brussels. Belgium became a battle ground and many of the wounded and injured were taken to Edith's hospital which was now being run by the Red Cross. The hospital aimed to be neutral treating the casualties from all sides with equal care and compassion.

Although Edith was nursing soldiers from the German, Belgium, French and British armies, she became involved in a scheme, led by Phillippe Baucq, which enabled over a hundred British and allied soldiers to escape to the Netherlands. While they were waiting for their escapes to be organised, many of the men were hidden in either Edith's house or hospital.

On 31 July 1915, Phillippe Baucq and a number of his fellow underground members were arrested by the German occupiers. Letters and betrayals also incriminated Edith and so she, too, was arrested a few days later even though she had helped treat and nurse many of the German army's wounded soldiers. There were even suspicions, never entirely proven, that she was also involved in spying for the Allied Forces.

After a short trial, on 11 October 1915, Edith and Phillippe were found guilty of treason by a German military court. A day later, they were taken to a firing range where they were shot dead. Edith was buried in a simple grave. Her story and tragic end quickly became international news and her execution led to widespread feelings of outrage.

In May 1919, when the war was over, Edith's body was exhumed. Such was the respect for Edith, both as a nurse and a brave woman, the service was attended by many dignitaries, including the King and Queen of Belgium. Her body was taken by boat and train to Westminster Abbey for a memorial service. Large, mournful crowds gathered along the routes. Again royalty was present in the person of the Queen Mother, Queen Adelaide. That same afternoon of 19 May, Edith's body was carried on its final journey back to Norwich for a service at the Cathedral. Edith Cavell was finally re-buried in a plot just outside the Cathedral's eastern walls in an area known as Life's Green. In 2016 Edith was honoured with a new grave, headstone and memorial garden planted with Edith Cavell roses.

Today she is remembered throughout the world. Many cities and towns have statues and memorial stones dedicated to her. Scores of hospital buildings, wards, schools, roads, streets, and gardens have been named after her, not only in her home city of Norwich but also in dozens of other cities and countries. There is a forty foot high memorial statue of her by Sir George Frampton sited in central London at the junction of St. Martin Place and Charing Cross Road just along the road from the church of St Martin's in the Field and Trafalgar Square where Nelson, that other Norfolk-born hero, can see her, with his good eye, from atop his column. Canada even named a mountain after her. Mount Edith Cavell, Alberta is 6585 feet high. And tumbling from its rocky slopes is the rather lovely and aptly named Angel Glacier.

In honour and memory of Miss Cavell and her role in helping soldiers escape, Edith became a popular name for girls in the years during and immediately after the First World

War, not just in Britain but in France, Belgium and several Commonwealth countries. Edith Piaf, the French cabaret singer, born in December 1915, a few months after the nurse's death, is perhaps the most famous of the many women to be named after the English nurse.

And so back to Edith's contemporary and county compatriot, Margaret Fountaine. Margaret's independence and passion have yet one more kindred spirit, perhaps not an obvious one at first glance, but someone whose star continues to rise. Like Margaret Fountaine and Edith Cavell, Julian of Norwich was a purposefully-minded, self-defining woman. However, whereas Margaret sought meaning and purpose by expanding her gaze to take in the whole world, Julian found meaning and purpose by narrowing her world to that of a single monastic cell.

We do not know much about Julian of Norwich, not even her true name. She was born around 1342, just a year before the birth of Geoffrey Chaucer author of *The Canterbury Tales* and William Langland who penned *The Vision of Piers Ploughman*. In the second half of her life she became an anchoress, that is someone who has withdrawn and retired from the world for religious and spiritual reasons.

The life of an anchoress, or anchorite is an ascetic one. She chooses to live the rest of her days in a single room or cell, often built against the wall of a church or monastery. Typically, the hermitage would have only three windows. One would open into the church so that the anchoress could hear mass. Another would allow servants to bring fresh food and clothes, and remove waste – of one kind and another. The third window usually faced the street allowing the anchoress to offer counsel and wisdom to anyone seeking her advice.

In general, anchorites commit themselves to prayer, devotional reading and the spiritual life. It was possible that

Julian took her name from St Julian's Church, Norwich, against which her cell was built. The original medieval church of St Julian's was bombed and completely destroyed in 1942, exactly 600 years after Julian's birth. However, in 1953, the church was rebuilt incorporating wherever possible a few ruined remains of the original church. The neat little building of flint and stone now stands on Kilderkin Way, Norwich, close to King Street and the River Wensum. And on its south side with entrance gained via the church is a replica of her cell. The church and its evocative addition attract visitors from all over the world. On a recent wander around the church, both inside and out, I heard a Canadian couple talking quietly about Julian's work and two Australian women discussing her life with one of the church guides.

In the 14th century, Norwich was a busy, thriving, crowded city, the second largest in England with its many churches and a sizeable population of around 13,000. Like all medieval towns, it was filthy, dirty, and smelly. It was also a time of plagues. Aged 30, Julian became seriously ill. The year was 1373. She writes:

> When I was thirty-and-a-half years old, God sent me an illness which held me for three days and three nights... And on the third night I often thought I was dying... And young as I was, I thought it was sad to die.

It was when she was feeling close to death that she experienced intense visions of Jesus and his suffering. During her visions – her 'shewings' – it became clear to her that God had a profound love of all humanity. Then she recovered.

Soon after her mystical experiences, Julian began to reflect on her visions and her revelations of the divine. The result was a manuscript titled *Revelations of Divine Love*, sometimes referred to by its original title, *The Shewings of Julian of Norwich*. The 'Short Text' as it's also called, is thought to be the first book ever written by a woman in English. It is rendered in the vernacular, in prose both beautiful and clear. Those skilled in these matters even recognise Julian's East Anglian accent coming through in the original hand-written, copied texts. Veronica Mary Rolf describes the book as the first-ever 'spiritual autobiography' in English.

Julian, now committed to the life of an anchoress, continued to reflect on her visions for the rest of her life. It is therefore interesting to note that in 1381, some ten years after her illness and while she was meditating on Christ's agonised, prolonged and bloody death, all around her the Peasants' Revolt was in full swing. This was a time of upheaval, violence and bloodshed.

Geoffrey Litester, the weaver of North Walsham, and his men were storming her city. Julian's bishop at the time was the 'fighting' Bishop of Norwich – Henry le Despencer. As we learned earlier, he was intent on quelling the Revolt. After Litester's capture, the Walsham weaver with his radical ideas was brought to the city where he was hung, drawn and bloodily quartered. These could be tricky times, even dangerous times for anyone who expressed unorthodox views, not just radical political views but also mystical and religious ones. Julian, with her visions and 'shewings', had to be circumspect.

Before Julian could formally take up the contemplative life of an anchoress she needed permission from her bishop who happened to be the same Henry le Despencer who had pursued the peasants and had their leaders killed. He needed to determine Julian's strength of body and mind. She had to be without debts; indeed have sufficient money to support herself, and possibly provide for at least one maid to prepare her meals, wash her cloths and take away her waste.

If satisfied, the bishop would perform the Rite of Enclosure followed by a Requiem Mass. In the event, Bishop le Despencer was satisfied and so Julian became an anchoress. She withdrew from the daily hub-bub, and confined herself to a single celled room built against the walls of the Church of St Julian. The troubled and the curious would visit her in her cell seeking guidance, advice or counsel. One of Julian's more interesting visitors was Margery Kempe. In need of advice about her own visions and what they might mean, Margery travelled to Norwich and spent several days talking with the aging anchoress, now nearing the end of her life.

Margery was born in 1373 in King's Lynn (then known as Bishop's Lynn), the daughter of a wealthy merchant family. Aged twenty, she married John Kempe with whom she had fourteen children. It was shortly after the birth of her first child that she began to have intense visions. But whereas Julian had but the one short series of visions upon which she meditated for the rest of her life, Margery had a lifetime of mystical conversations with Jesus and God. In her early forties, and after her meeting with Julian, as well as reading the works of another mystic, Bridget of Sweden, she left her husband and became a pilgrim, yet another Norfolk walker. She journeyed to the Holy Land, throughout Europe, and across much of England. In 1436 towards the end of her own life and no doubt inspired by Julian's writings, Margery, the Christian mystic, dictated her own book, *The Book of Margery Kempe*. It describes her life, visions, pilgrimages and preachings. It was one of the earliest autobiographies to be written in English. Margery died two years later in 1438.

It seems likely that Margery not only read Julian's writings but might even have possessed a copy of them. It was during her years as a recluse that Julian wrote a longer version of *Revelations of Divine Love* in which she explored further and more deeply the meaning of her visions and her spiritual and religious experiences. The book was 63,500 words long and made up of 86 separate chapters. Initially, only a few copies of the 'Long Text', as it became known, were in circulation, limited mainly to the libraries of monasteries and convents.

It was later thought that most copies were either lost or destroyed around the late 1630s when Henry VIII was busy dissolving and destroying the country's monasteries, including their libraries. However, in the 1660s, a copy of Julian's book was known to be in the Bibliothéque Nationale in Paris. An English Benedictine monk, Serenus de Cressy, working as a chaplain at a convent in Cambria, northern France, made a visit to the Paris library and came across Julian's *Revelations of Divine Love*. The copy he read was hand-written. Serenus decided to publish the first-ever printed edition which appeared in 1670. But even then, the book remained largely unknown and unread.

Sir Hans Sloane, after whom Sloane Square in London is named, was a doctor and a scientist. He was a collector of paintings and drawing, rocks and coins, flora and fauna, books and manuscripts. Like Sir Thomas Browne, he ended up with a vast 'cabinet of curiosities'.

On his death in 1753, he bequeathed the whole of his collection to the Nation. Along with books donated from the Library of King George II, Sloane's collection formed the basis of what was to become the British Museum which first opened its doors to the public in 1759. The rocks, flora and fauna, although initially housed with the books at the British Museum, eventually found their way elsewhere. Their seminal role was to be in the creation of the Natural History Museum, whose original name was actually the British Museum (Natural History), reflecting its parentage.

Among the thousands of books left to the newly established British Museum were two copies of the Benedictine monk's printed version of Julian's *Revelations*. It is not known how often the book was read, if at all, as it lay somewhere in the Museum. However, a hundred years later, at least one person discovered and read Julian's writings and decided that they needed a wider audience. In 1877, the Reverend Henry Collins brought out a brand new edition of the Long Text, based on Serenus de Cressy's 1660s' printed copy. But even this refresher didn't appear to do much to boost Julian's book or reputation, though Florence Nightingale was said to have taken a copy with her to the Crimea.

The turning point came in 1901. Methuen, the publishers, brought out a new edition of the *Revelations of Divine Love*. It was edited by Grace Warrack, about whom not much is known other than she was a Scottish woman, born in 1855 and who died in Edinburgh in 1932. The quality of her editing was first class. Grace had written an introduction that was both scholarly and thoughtful with many helpful footnotes and cross-references.

The edition was a great success and remains in print today. It marked the beginning of a full appreciation of Julian's importance as a thinker, mystic philosopher, and writer. She has influenced a wide range of theologians, people of faith, novelists and poets, perhaps most famously T. S. Eliot who quotes her at the end of his poem, *Little Gidding*, the fourth of his Four Quartets. It took over 500 years for the *Revelations* to attract significant interest and attention. And since then, Julian's words and wisdom have spread far and wide with translations into many languages.

Margaret Fountaine travelled the world to find fulfilment. In contrast, Julian stopped moving. She took her *self* to a cell, a few yards square, but she, too, found joy and meaning. It was her words of love that were destined to travel while she stayed still. She died in around 1416, aged seventy four.

Julian's theology was unusual, even radical for the time. She was excited by the idea of a loving, compassionate, merciful, forgiving, more maternal God, a God less severe, masculine, judgemental, punitive and wrathful. 'God is the goodness that cannot be angry,' she writes, 'for he is nothing but goodness.' Her spiritual influence and significance have slowly grown over the centuries. There is a statue of her holding the *Revelations of Divine Love* perched on the left hand outside wall of the main doors of Norwich Cathedral. (See *Plate 20*) Adjacent, on the right hand side of the doors, is a statue of the Cathedral's founder and first bishop, Hebert de Losinga.

Julian's home city of Norwich also organises a week-long festival in her honour. It is a time of music, talks and workshops.

There is much discussion of her spiritual writings, the power of retreat to focus the mind, and her implicit feminist sympathies. 'Just because I am a woman,' she says, 'why must I not write of the goodness of God.' The festival revels in the wonder of her reflections as she reports the words of Jesus as she heard them in her visions, the same words of hope that Eliot incorporates in the final poem of his Quartet:

> All shall be well, and all shall be well, and all manner
> of things shall be well.

In the end, whatever happens, it's going to be all right. There is a deep optimism in the writings of both Julian and Margaret Fountaine. 'All shall be well,' says Julian. 'I want to see all I can of this beautiful world before I leave it,' records Margaret, and so she pursues her love of butterflies.

Butterflies, of course, are that most beautiful and yet symbolically ephemeral of things. Their moment can be as brief as a day, but what a glorious day. They are the souls of the dead, the jewels of the air. Butterflies have attracted some of the most avid collectors and enthusiasts over the centuries. The lepidopterists. The Aurelians. The butterfly people.

Patrick Barkham is a journalist and natural history writer. He was born in Norfolk which is where again he now lives. He is the author of a growing number of books, including *The Butterfly Isles: a summer in search of our emperors and admirals*. His only mention of his county compatriot, Margaret Fountaine, is at the very end in a bibliography. But their shared passion is evident.

In 2009, in the course of a single summer Patrick set out to find and see, in the wild, every one of Britain's 59 species of butterfly. The mission was triggered by the childhood adventures he had had with his dad. They shared a love of butterflies. They hatched a plan to try and see as many different British species as they could, believed then to number fifty-eight. Eventually they 'ran out of summers, or steam' and got stuck at fifty-four.

But the lepidopteral lure didn't go away. Approaching his fortieth year, Patrick decided that he must complete the 'unfinished business.' And so in that early summer of 2009, he started his quest to 'unlock the ordinary, everyday beauty of the natural world.' He was also driven by fears of the alarming decline in the number of butterflies reported year on year.

Like most modern butterfly enthusiasts, he did not kill and pin his specimens to a display board. Instead he described and photographed them in exquisite detail. And as is often the case with natural historians, nature also prompted him to reflect on life's wider and deeper themes.

It was after a long search that he finally came across the small, misty Wood White – in a wood, of course – in Surrey. It was hanging on a leaf and was 'the shape of a droplet of water'. But the find also inspired an understanding, an insight. The delicate, fragile, momentarily motionless butterfly with its wings closed, thought Patrick, has 'the ability just to be, and live fully in the present.' Like the butterfly, sometimes we need to live in the moment and simply go with the flow.

Although the language and the context are different, Patrick's reflections echo those recorded by Julian of Norwich over six hundred years earlier as she pondered her visions of Jesus. She saw three properties of God: life, love and light. 'In life is marvellous homelyhed, in love is gentle courtesy, and in light is endless being.' In her 'revelations' she is struck by the thought that God loves us and enfolds us; that everything is good. She wonders why there is anything at all, and concludes that it is God's love that brings everything into being.

> And then he showed me a little thing, the size of a hazelnut, in the palm of my hand; and it was as round as a ball. I looked in my mind's eye and I thought:

'What may this be?' And answer came: 'It is all that is made.' I marvelled that it could last, for I thought it might have crumbled to nothing, it was so small. And the answer came into my mind: 'It lasts, and ever shall, because God loves it.' And so all things have being through the love of God.

Of the fifty-nine butterflies initially sought by Patrick, eleven were eventually found in his home county of Norfolk. And the very first one he saw that year was spotted in Sheringham, in his mum's garden on the 15 March 2009. The garden pond was an orgy of mating frogs. Patrick crept up on the seething mass. First they froze. Then they flopped below the water. 'All was still. And then I saw the Small Tortoiseshell.' It was on a rock by the edge of the pond, sunning itself. It is one of our more common, familiar butterflies and with its distinctive colouring of autumnal reds and browns, oranges and blacks, and its dabs of white and blue, the little butterfly can be seen in most gardens throughout the spring and summer. So began Patrick's quest.

Only an hour later his mum motions him to come outside again. And there is his second butterfly, a Brimstone – the ancient name for sulphur, pale yellow with a greenish tinge. Sheringham. A good start for Patrick. And only a mile north and west of Beacon Hill where my own wanderings began, three hundred and thirty eight feet high looking out over the sea, sands and shingle of North Norfolk.

This is a coastline in retreat, a retreat 'managed' by The Environment Agency, defended in stretches by sea walls and salt marshes, but otherwise vulnerable, defenceless, frayed, time-limited, beautiful. Where the coast is exposed, heavy rains and high seas de-stabilise the sandy clay cliffs. They slip, slide and quickly disappear into the grey waters below, lost forever, barely a memory. In a lovely poem, Blake Morrison blames East Anglia's coastal erosion on its dead sailors and fishermen as they yearn to be back at sea and escape their earthy graves:

The tides go in and out
But the cliffs are stuck in reverse:
Back across the fields they creep,
to the graves of Covehithe church

From church to beach
Was once a hike.
Today it's just a stroll.
Soon it'll be a stone's throw.

And that path we took
Along the cliffs has itself been taken,
By winter storms.
The wheat's living on the edge.

What's to be done?
I blame the dead
in their grassy mounds,
the sailors and the fishermen

longing to be back at sea
who since they can't get up
and stride down the beach
entice the sea to come to them.

It's summer. The view out to sea from Beacon Hill is a little hazy.
There is no breeze. I see a butterfly, a hedge brown, also known
as a gatekeeper because of its habit of fluttering around field
gates and meadow walls. It's not a rare butterfly, but no less
exquisite for all that. It darts staccato over the grass and scrub.
It settles for a moment. It is small but subtly coloured in brushes
of orange and gold with wings edged in milk chocolate brown
and eye-spots of black on each wing pricked with two tiny dots
of white. And then off it goes, zigging and zagging on its way.

The gatekeeper will live for a week or two as it flits over the summer flowers growing on the 430,000-year-old sands and clays of Beacon Hill, the debris of a once vast ice sheet, long since gone. But the hill's days, too, are numbered. In a few thousand years, Beacon Hill, still Norfolk's highest point, will become Norfolk's highest cliff as the North Sea wears and tears its way south, metre by metre, year after year. And a few thousand years after that it, too, will be gone.

Seas rise and fall. Lands appear and disappear. Mountains come and go. Each species has its day before reaching the end of its evolutionary branch on the tree of life. The tectonic plates continue to inch their stately way over the planet's surface. Slowly, imperceptibly the Earth's geography changes. What we now call The British Isles will continue their journey north, riding the north-western edges of the great Eurasian plate a few centimetres each year, at least for a while, before the mantle's deep, hot, viscous conveyor belt carries them off who knows where. And way, way into the future, 5 billion years from now, the show will be over.

In its very old age, our sun will cool and slacken. Its pressure will fall and density thin. It will grow bigger and bigger. Astronomers call these dying stars red giants. In its final bloated state, our sun will expand further and further outwards, evaporating the solar system's inner planets one by one. First Mercury. Followed by Venus. And then the Earth. Our 10 billion year old planet will boil away and be no more.

But here I am, watching a butterfly, in Norfolk, on a hill which, geologically speaking, barely registers. Soon it will be no more, leaving not a trace. I'm having my brief moment in the light, exquisitely aware of so much time, so much space, so much beauty. Better make the most of it.

About the author

David Howe has lived and worked in Norfolk for over forty years. Although he has always been a keen walker, since retiring from the University of East Anglia his wanderings in the county have become even more regular and reflective.

Acknowledgements

After a career writing academic books, I was unsure what the world might make of my attempt to write a more generalised work of non-fiction. It was inspired by my love of walking and more specifically by my wanderings around Norfolk. I ploughed on, not exactly writing in secret, but as a private pleasure. But after a couple of drafts I needed the book to be read by others who might cast a more critical eye over the project. So huge thanks to Catherine Gray, friend and publisher, who was the first to read the draft manuscript and give her usual wise and sound counsel.

Chris Beckett, friend and successful author of a growing number of highly regarded science fiction novels, also read my initial efforts. Chris, many thanks for your insights and expertise. And gratitude to another Chris. Chris Rushby is the book buyer for Jarrold's store in Norwich. He might not remember but he gave me really useful information about local publishers who might be interested in the kind of book I had written. One of his suggestions was Mousehold Press, based in Norwich. This led me to the publisher himself, Adrian Bell. Adrian's interest, support and guidance has been wonderful. A big thank you Adrian, and to Chris for pointing me in the direction of Mousehold Press.

Dr David Waterhouse of Norfolk Museums Service based in Norwich Castle was good enough to answer my questions about Margaret Fountaine and her butterfly collection as well as track down the photograph of her holding her bicycle. Thanks, too, to Jeremiah Solak of London Science Museum's Science and Society Picture Library who found the photograph of Einstein by his hut on Roughton Heath and explained how we might reproduce it in the book.

Mike Page, Aerial Photographer (Mike-Page.co.uk) has kindly allowed me to use three of the many wonderful aerial photographs that he has taken above the skies of

Norfolk. Thanks Mike. Thanks also to Terry Loan for the maps of Norfolk that appear at the beginning of the book.

Blake Morrison, on behalf of his publisher, Chatto and Windus, has kindly given me permission to quote his evocative poem, Covehithe, one of many wonderful poems in his splendid book *Shingle Street* (of which I now have a signed copy!).

I also owe a considerable debt of gratitude to the Norfolk and Norwich's Millennium Library and the University of East Anglia's library. This book would not have been possible without them. They provided the papers and books upon which much of the research for *Wandering in Norfolk* is based. And a final thanks to the librarians whose patience and ever-friendly guidance helped me find what I was looking for, however old, obscure or dusty. Any errors, of fact or judgement, of course, remain entirely mine.

David Howe
Norwich

Bibliography

Abel, Christine (2005) 'The Havens of North Norfolk', in Ian Scott (ed.) *The Turn of the Tide: North Norfolk's Saltmarsh Coast*, Fakenham: JJG Publishing.

Ashton, N., Lewis, S., de Grotter, I. et al (2014), Hominin Footprints from Early Pleistocene Deposits at Happisburgh, UK, PLoS One Feb 7 (9(2) doi 10.1371/journal.pone.0088329.eCollection.

Baggini, Julian (2004) *What's It All About? Philosophy and the meaning of life*. London: Granta Books.

Barkham, Patrick (2010), *The Butterfly Isles: A Summer in Search of Our Emperors and Admirals*, London: Granta.

Barkham, Patrick (2015), 'Do we like to be beside the seaside?' *Guardian: Family*, 4 April p 3.

BBC Radio 4: *Emma Turner: a life in the reeds*, 26 January 2012

Blackburn, Julia (2015), *Threads: The Delicate Life of John Craske*, London: Jonathan Cape.

Borrow, George (1851), *Lavengro: The Scholar, the Gypsy, the Priest*, Edinburgh: John Murray.

Borrow, George (1857), *The Romany Rye*, Edinburgh: John Murray

Browne, Thomas (1658) *Pseudodoxia Epidemica: Enquiries into Very Many Received Tenets and Commonly Preformed Truths, London: Edward Dod.*

Browne, Thomas (1658), *Hydriotaphia: Urne Buriall*, London: Henry Brome.

Callaway, Ewen (2015), UK mapped out by genetic ancestry, *Nature*, 19 March.

Cocker, Mark (2015), 'Country Diary', *Guardian* 17 Feb. p 44.

Deakin, Roger (2000), *Waterlog: A Swimmer's Journey Through Britain*, London: Vintage.

Dobson, Richard B. (1970), *The Peasants' Revolt of 1381*, Bath: Pitman

Eagleton, Terry (2008), *The Meaning of Life: A Very Short Introduction*. Oxford: Oxford University Press.

Eyers, Jill (1998), *Rocks Afoot: Geology of North East Norfolk*, High Wycombe: Eyers.

Farrant, Ann (2014), *Amelia Opie: The Quaker Celebrity*, Hindringham: JJG.

Fountaine, Margaret (1980), *Love Among the Butterflies: The Travels and Adventures of a Victorian Lady*. Edited by W. F. Cater, London: Collins

Fountaine, Margaret (1986). *Butterflies and Late Loves: The Further Adventures of a Victorian Lady, Edited by W. F. Cater, London: Collins.*

Fry, Elizabeth (1847), *Memoir of the Life of Elizabeth Fry: extracts from her journal and letters, London: Charles Gilpin.*

Goodman, Anthony (2002), *Margery Kempe and Her World*, London: Longman.

Gros, Frédéric (2014), *A Philosophy of Walking*, New York: Verso

Hingley, Richard and Unwin, Christine (2005), *Boudica: Iron Age Warrior Queen, London: Hambledon Continuum.*

Holmes, Richard (1985), *Footsteps: Adventures of a Romantic Biographer*, London: Harper Perennial.

Keane, John (!995), *Tom Paine: A Political Life*, London: Bloomsbury

Larwood, G. P. and Furnell, B. M. (1970), *The Geology of Norfolk*, Norwich: Geological Society of Norfolk.

Leslie, Stephen et al (2015), The fine-scale genetic structure of the UK population, *Nature:* 519, pp 309-14.

Linebaugh, Peter (2014), *Stop Thief: The Commons, Enclosures and Resistance*, P.M. Press, Oakland: CA.

Lister, Adrian and Stuart, Anthony (2010), The West Runton mammoth: mammus trogonthereii and its evolutionary significance, *Quaternary International*, Vol. 228 (1-2), pp 180-209.

Macfarlane, Robert (2003), *Mountains of the Mind: A History of a Fascination, London: Granta Books.*Macfarlane, Robert (2008), *The Wild Places*, London: Granta Publications.

Macfarlane, Robert (2013), *The Old Ways*, London: Penguin Books

Mansfied, H. O. (1976), *Norfolk Churches: Their Foundations, Architecture and Furnishings*, Lavenham: Terence Dalton Limited

Mitchell, Laurence (2014), *Norfolk: Slow Travel, Local, Characterful Guides to Britain's Special Places*, Chalfont St Peter, Bucks.: Bradt Travel Guides Ltd.

Moorlock, B.S.P. (2002), *Geology of the Cromer District: a brief explanation of the geological map sheet 131 Cromer*, Nottingham: British Geological Survey.

Morrison, Blake (2015), Covehithe, The Saturday Poem, *Guardian Review*, Saturday, 21 January, p 18.

Morrison, Blake (2015), *Shingle Street*, London: Chatto and Windus

Nicholson, Geoff (2011), *The Lost Art of Walking: The History, Science, Philosophy, Literature, Theory and Practice of Pedestrianism*, Chelmsford: Harbour Books.

North Norfolk Coastal Partnership (2011), *Geological Landscapes of the Norfolk Coast*, Fakenham: North Norfolk Coastal Partnership

Paine, Thomas (1791-2/1993), *The Rights of Man*, London: Everyman Library, J.M. Dent.

Preston, Claire (2005), *Thomas Browne and the Writing of Early Modern Science*, Cambridge: Cambridge University Press.

Parry, James (2011), 'Broadland's Bittern Pioneer', *Tern*, Summer, p 7.

Pevsner, Nikolaus and Wilson, Bill (1997), *The Buildings of England: Norfolk 1: Norwich and North East*, London: Penguin.

Pevsner, Nikolaus and Wilson, Bill (1999), *The Buildings of England: Norfolk 2: North West and South*, London: Penguin.

Powell, Edgar (1896), *The Rising in East Anglia in 1381*, Cambridge: Cambridge UP.

Quinlan, Ray (2003) *The Greater Ridgeway*, Milnethorpe, Cumbria: Cicerone Press.

Raban, Jonathan (1987), *For Love and Money*, New York: Harper Collins.

Ramirez, Janina (2016), *Julian of Norwich: A Very Brief History*, London: SPCK.

Rickman, Thomas Clio (1819), *The Life of Thomas Paine*, London

Rolf, Veronica Mary (2013), *Julian's Gospel: Illuminating the Life and Revelations of Julian of Norwich*, Marknoll, New York: Orbis Books

Saul, Nigel (1999), *Richard II*, New Haven, Yale UP, p 74.

Sebald, W. G. (2002), *The Rings of Saturn*, London: Vintage Books

Sebald, W. G. (2006), *Campo Santo*, London: Penguin.

Shepherd, Nan (2011), *The Living Mountain*, Edinburgh: Canongate

Skipper, Keith (2011), *Come Yew On, Tergether: A rich crop of Norfolk dialect writing*, Norwich: Mousehold Press.

Souhami, Diana (2015), *Edith Cavell: Nurse, Martyr, Heroine*, Riverun

Stevenson, Robert Louis (1879/1907), *Travels with a Donkey in the Cevennes*, London: Chatto and Windus.

Sugden, John (2004), *Nelson: A Dream of Glory*, London: Pimlico

Taylor, John, Childs, Wendy and Watkiss, Leslie (eds.) (2011), *The St Albans Chronicle: The Chronica Maiiora of Thomas Walsingham Volume I: 1376-1394*, Oxford: Clarendon Press.

Thomas, Edward (1905), *Beautiful Wales,* Oxford: A. & C. Black

Thomas, Edward (1912), *George Borrow: The Man and his Books*, London: Chapman Hall.

Thomas, Edward (1916), *The Icknield Way*, London: Constable.

Turner, Emma (1924), *Broadland Birds,* London: Country Life.

Turner, Emma (1928), *Bird Watching on Scolt Head*, London: Country Life.

UEA Film, Media and Television (2014): *Norfolk Women in History Timeline*. Interview with Dr Tony Irwin (2014), Senior Curator of Natural History, Norfolk Museums and Archaelogy Service

Upjohn, Sheila (2007), *In Search of Julian of Norwich*, Harrisburg, NY: Morehouse Publishing.

Waring, Sophie (2015), Margaret Fountaine: a lepidopterist remembered, *Notes and Records*, 20 March, Vol. 69(1).

Webster, Graham (1993), *Boudica: The British Revolt Against Rome AD 60,* London: Routledge.

Williams, Kate (2007), *England's Mistress: The Infamous Life of Emma Hamilton*, London: Arrow.

Wood, Andy (2002), *Riot, Rebellion and Popular Politics in Early Modern England*, Basingstoke: Palgrave.

Wood, Andy (2004), Kett's Rebellion. In C. Rawcliffe and R. Wilson (eds) *Medieval Norwich*, London: Hambledon and London, pp 277-300.